C000134413

BRITISH TYPE 2 DIABETES COOKBOOK 2024

130 Easy, Delicious & Low-Carbs Recipes With a 28-Day Meal Plan

TABLE OF CONTENTS

FRUIT RECIPES 46

LAMB RECIPES 62

PORK RECIPES 70

VEGETABLES RECIPES 75

INTRODUCTION

TYPE 1 DIABETES

If you have type 1 diabetes, your blood sugar is too high because your body can't make a hormone called insulin. Fewer than one in 10 people in the UK who have diabetes have type 1 diabetes. There is nothing you can do to prevent yourself or others developing type 1 diabetes. The exact causes are not known. Although it's often diagnosed in childhood, people can develop type 1 diabetes at any age. You are at a slightly higher risk of type 1 diabetes if your mother, father, brother or sister has it. Insulin is the main treatment for type 1 diabetes. You can't live without insulin injections or using an insulin pump. Checking and managing your blood sugar levels is important to help you reduce your risk of serious short or long-term health problems. These are called diabetes complications. There is currently no cure for type 1 diabetes, but we're funding lots of research to help find new treatments and a cure.

TYPE 2 DIABETES

Type 2 diabetes is the most common type. It is high blood sugar levels due to your body not making enough of a hormone called insulin, or what it makes not working properly — known as insulin resistance. Treatment includes eating well and moving more. Some people may also need to take diabetes medication such as metformin or insulin. Type 2 diabetes can go undiagnosed for years if symptoms are missed. Left untreated high blood sugar levels can cause serious health problems called diabetes complications. Anyone can develop type 2 diabetes but it mostly affects people over 25 often with a family history. Type 2 diabetes doesn't just affect people living with overweight or obesity, although this is one of the risk factors, along with ethnicity. There's no cure but some people with type 2 diabetes can put their diabetes into remission by losing a significant amount of weight.

WHAT ARE THE SIGNS AND SYMPTOMS OF DIABETES?

Are you worried that you, your child or someone you know may have diabetes? Having some diabetes symptoms doesn't mean you definitely have the condition, but you should always contact your GP, just to make sure.

Diabetes symptoms

- Toilet - going for a wee a lot, especially at night.

- Thirsty - being really thirsty.

- Tired - feeling more tired than usual.

- Thinner - losing weight without trying to.

- Genital itching or thrush.

- Cuts and wounds take longer to heal.

- Blurred eyesight

- Increased hunger.

These symptoms can affect anyone - adult or child. But some are more commonly experienced by people with type 1 diabetes, and can come on really quickly.

WHAT ARE THE MOST COMMON SYMPTOMS?

No individual is the same. You may also experience other symptoms and the symptoms you have may not exactly match that of another person and may not be on the list above. However, the most common symptoms experienced by many people with diabetes are increased thirst, going for a wee a lot, feeling tired and losing weight.

HOW DO YOU REVERSE DIABETES?

The strongest evidence we have at the moment suggests that type 2 diabetes is mainly put into remission by weight loss. Remission is more likely if you lose weight as soon as possible after your diabetes diagnosis. However, we do know of people who have put their diabetes into remission 25 years after diagnosis. If you have obesity, your diabetes is more likely to go into remission if you lose a substantial amount of weight – 15kg (or 2 stone 5lbs) – as quickly and safely as possible following diagnosis. It's important to know that not everyone who loses this much weight will be able to put their diabetes into remission. But losing 15kg comes with a lot of health benefits, even if you don't lead to remission. Research shows that getting support to lose just 5% of your body weight can have huge benefits for your health. Losing extra weight can lead to:

- fewer medications
- better blood sugar levels
- a lower risk of complications.

Things like your age, ethnicity and family history can all contribute to your overall risk. We also know that having obesity is the most significant risk factor. If you know you have obesity, losing weight is one way you can prevent type 2 diabetes. And eating a healthy, balanced diet is way great way to manage your weight. Any amount of weight loss can help, research shows losing even 1kg can help to reduce your risk. There are so many different ways to lose weight, so it's important to find out what works best for you. We know that not everyone who is at risk or living with diabetes type 2 diabetes is carrying extra weight. But whether you need to lose weight or not, it is still important to make healthier food choices. Research tells us that there are even certain foods that are linked to reducing the risk of type 2 diabetes. Here are our top tips for healthier food choices you can make, to reduce your risk of type 2 diabetes.

1. Choose drinks without added sugar

We know there is a link between having full sugar fizzy and energy drinks, and an increased risk of type 2 diabetes. Cutting down on these can help to reduce your risk and support keeping your weight down. Evidence also shows that drinking unsweetened tea and coffee is associated with a reduced risk. If you are finding it hard to cut down, look out for diet or low calorie versions of soft drinks and check there's no added sugar. Try not to replace sugary drinks with fruit juices or smoothies as these still contain a high amount of free sugar. Try plain water, plain milk, tea or coffee without added sugar, as replacements.

2. Choose higher fibre carbs

Eating white bread, white rice and sugary breakfast cereals known as refined carbs are linked with an increased risk of type 2 diabetes. But wholegrains such as brown rice, wholewheat pasta, wholemeal flour, wholegrain bread and oats and linked to a reduced risk so choose these instead. When you're out shopping remember to check food labels to see if a food is high fibre. Compare different foods to find the ones with the most fibre in them.

Other healthy sources of carbs include:

- fruit and vegetables
- pulses such has chickpeas, beans and lentils
- dairy like unsweetened yoghurt and milk

Having more fibre is also associated with lower risk of other serious conditions such as obesity, heart diseases and certain types of cancers. It's also important to think about your carbohydrate portion sizes.

3. Cut down on red and processed meat

Having more red and processed meats like bacon, ham, sausages, pork, beef and lamb are all associated with an increased risk of type 2 diabetes. They also have links to heart problems and certain types of cancer.

Try to get your protein from healthier foods like:

- pulses such as beans and lentils
- eggs
- fish
- chicken and turkey
- unsalted nuts

Fish is really good for us and oily fish like salmon and mackerel are rich in omega-3 oil which helps protect your heart. Try to have at least one portion of oily fish each week and one portion of white fish.

4. Eat plenty of fruit and veg

Including more fruit and vegetables in your diet is linked with a reduced risk of type 2 diabetes. But did you know there are also certain types of fruit and veg that have been specifically associated with a reduced risk?

These are:

- apples
- grapes
- berries
- green leafy veg such as spinach, kale, watercress, rocket.

It doesn't matter whether they are fresh or frozen, try to find ways to include these in your diet. Try having them as snacks or an extra portion of veg with your meals.   It can be confusing to know whether you should eat certain types of fruit, because they contain sugar. The good news is the natural sugar in whole fruit is not the type of added (or free) sugar we need to cut down on. But drinks like fruit juices and smoothies do contain free sugar, so eat the whole fruit and veg instead.

5. Choose unsweetened yogurt and cheese

Yogurt and cheese are fermented dairy products and they have been linked with a reduced risk of type 2 diabetes. You might be wondering whether to choose full fat or low fat? When it comes to dairy and risk of type 2 diabetes, the amount of fat from these dairy foods is not as important. What is more important is that you choose unsweetened options like plain natural or Greek yoghurt and plain milk.

Having three portions of dairy each day also helps you to get the calcium your body needs. A portion of dairy is:

- 200ml (1/3 pint) milk
- 30g cheese
- 125g yoghurt

6. Be sensible with alcohol

Drinking too much alcohol is linked with an increased risk of type 2 diabetes. As it is also high in calories, drinking lots can make it difficult if you are trying to lose weight. Current guidelines recommend not regularly drinking more than 14 units per week and that these units should be spread evenly over 3-4 days. Try to have a few days per week without any alcohol at all).   Drinking heavily on one or two days per week, known as binge drinking, will also increase the risk of other health conditions such as certain types of cancer.

7. Choose healthier snacks

If you want a snack, go for things like:

- unsweetened yoghurts
- unsalted nuts
- seeds
- fruits and vegetables

instead of crisps, chips, biscuits, sweets and chocolates. But watch your portions as it'll help you keep an eye on your weight.

8. Include healthier fats in your diet

It's important to have some healthy fat in our diets because it gives us energy. The type of fat we choose can affect our health. Some saturated fats can increase the amount of cholesterol in your blood, increasing your risk of heart problems. These are mainly found in animal products and prepared food like:

- red and processed meat
- butter
- lard
- ghee
- biscuits, cakes, sweets, pies and pastries.

If you are at risk of type 2 diabetes, you are likely to be at an increased risk of heart problems so try to reduce these foods.

Healthier fats are found in foods like:

- unsalted nuts
- seeds
- avocados

Savoury Meatloaf And Onion Gravy

Servings: 6

Cooking Time: 1.5 Hours

Ingredients:

- For the meatloaf:
- 225g lean minced beef
- 225g lean minced pork
- Breadcrumbs made with 1 ½ slices medium wholemeal bread
- 2 tbsp chopped fresh mixed herbs (parsley, thyme, oregano)
- 1 small red onion, finely chopped
- 1 medium eating apple, grated
- 1 tsp ground black pepper
- For the onion gravy:
- 2 red onions, finely sliced
- calorie-controlled cooking spray
- 4 tsp reduced salt gravy granules made with ½ pint (285ml) water
- 1 tsp wholegrain mustard
- 1 tbsp finely chopped fresh chives

Directions:

1. Preheat the oven to 190°C/gas 5. Mix all the meatloaf ingredients together in a large bowl and season to taste.

2. Press the mixture into a 450g loaf tin. Cover with foil and bake in the oven for 1¼ hours until cooked through.

3. Meanwhile, to make the onion gravy, heat a non-stick pan, add the onions with three sprays of low calorie spray and dry-fry over a moderate heat until the onions start to brown. Add ½ pint of cold water and stir. Mix the gravy powder in a separate jug with 2 tbsp cold water and stir into the pan.

4. Simmer gently to thicken, adding more water if required, then stir in the mustard and chives. Delicious poured over the meatloaf.

Recipe Tips

You could make this in individual ramekins, which will cook more quickly in around 1 hour.

If you don't have a loaf tin, mould the mixture into a loaf shape on a baking tray, cover the top and sides with foil and bake.

This can be made with all pork or all beef mince, if you prefer.

Freezing instructions: Suitable for freezing once cooked. Defrost thoroughly in the fridge or microwave and reheat until piping-hot throughout.

Nutrition:

KCal 180   Carbs 12.7g   Fibre 2.7g   Protein 19.5g

Fat 5.1g   Saturates 2.1g   Sugars 7.1g   Salt 0.46g

Fruit/Veg Portion 0

Oriental Beef Stir-Fry

Servings: 4

Cooking Time: 8-10 Minutes

Ingredients:

- 2 tsp vegetable oil
- 400g lean beef steak (rump or sirloin)
- 4 cloves garlic, crushed
- 2 yellow or red peppers deseeded and sliced
- 200g broccoli, cut into small florets
- 4 spring onions, sliced
- 2 pak choi (bok choy), sliced
- 1 small tin (200g) water chestnuts, drained and sliced
- 2 tbsp oyster sauce

Directions:

1. Heat the oil in a non-stick frying pan or wok. Trim any fat from the steak, cut into thin strips and add to the pan.

2. Stir-fry for 1–2 minutes to seal, add the garlic, peppers, broccoli florets and spring onions, along with 2 tbsp water.

3. Stir fry for 3 minutes, add the pak choi, water chestnuts and oyster sauce. Allow to heat through thoroughly and serve immediately.

Recipe Tips

You could use lean pork or chicken in place of beef.

For a veggie version, use firm tofu cut into strips. Fry for 3–4 mins each side then remove from the pan, cook the rest of the ingredients, add the tofu back, mix well and serve.

Nutrition:

KCal 214   Carbs 10.0g   Fibre 4.9g   Protein 26.9g

Fat 6.3g   Saturates 2.0g   Sugars 6.3g   Salt 1.01g

Fruit/Veg Portion 2

Moussaka

Servings: 6

Cooking Time: 90 Minutes

Ingredients:

- 3 aubergines, thinly sliced (approx 3/4cm)
- 1 tsp rapeseed oil
- 2 medium onions, finely chopped
- 500g lean minced beef
- 1 red pepper, finely chopped
- 1 carrot, grated
- 3 cloves garlic, chopped
- 400g can tomatoes
- 1 tbsp tomato puree
- 1 tsp oregano
- 1 tsp ground cinnamon
- 1 low-salt beef stock cube, dissolved in 100ml boiling water
- For the topping:
- 200g 0% fat Greek yogurt
- 50g reduced-fat Cheddar, finely grated
- 1 heaped tsp ground nutmeg

Directions:

1. Preheat the oven 180°C/gas 4. Grill the aubergine slices for 3-4 minutes on each side and set aside.

2. Heat the oil in a pan and add the onions. When they

start to brown, add the minced beef and stir for 5 minutes, breaking up any clumps with a wooden spoon.

3. Add the red pepper and carrot and cook for 5 minutes then stir in the garlic, tomatoes, purée, oregano and cinnamon.

4. Stir in the stock, bring to the boil then turn down the heat, cover and simmer for 10-15 minutes.

5. Meanwhile, make the topping mix the yogurt, Cheddar and nutmeg together.

6. In an ovenproof dish, place a layer of aubergine, add a spoonful of the beef mixture then layer alternately, ending with a layer of aubergine.

7. Spoon the yogurt mixture over the top and bake for 45 minutes.

Recipe Tips

Leave to cool for 15-20 minutes before serving.

Moussaka is often made with minced lamb. For a lower-fat version use minced turkey instead.

Freezing instructions: Suitable for freezing once cooked. Defrost in the fridge or microwave and reheat until piping hot throughout.

Nutrition:

KCal 216   Carbs 10.3g   Fibre 4.9g   Protein 26.4g
Fat 6.6g   Saturates 3.2g   Sugars 8.9g   Salt 0.4g
Fruit/Veg Portion 2

Minced Beef And Vegetable Filo Pie

Servings: 4

Cooking Time: 35 Minutes

Ingredients:

- 1 tsp rapeseed oil
- 1 onion, diced
- 100g mushrooms, chopped
- 250g lean minced beef
- 1 carrot, diced small
- 150g sweet potato, peeled and diced into small pieces
- 2 tsp plain flour
- 1 tsp tomato puree
- good pinch white pepper
- pinch dried thyme
- 1 reduced-salt beef stock cube, dissolved in 300ml water
- 75g defrosted frozen peas
- 2 sprays rapeseed oil
- 150g filo pastry (approx. 3 sheets)

Directions:

1. Preheat the oven to 180°C/gas 4. Heat the oil in a saucepan, add the onions and stir until lightly browned.

2. Add the mushrooms and minced beef and stir for 4-5 minutes breaking up any clumps of meat with a wooden spoon.

3. Add the diced carrot and sweet potato, sprinkle with the flour and mix well. Stir in the tomato puree, pepper and thyme.

4. Stir in the stock, bring to the boil, cover with the pan lid, reduce the heat and simmer for 12-15 minutes until the carrots are tender. Add the peas, stir and place the mixture in an ovenproof dish.

5. Spray a little oil onto the filo sheets and put slightly 'scrunched' layers on top of the beef mixture.

6. Bake for 10 minutes until the pastry is lightly browned. Serve with steamed carrots, corn and broccoli.

Nutrition:

KCal 316   Carbs 39.6g   Fibre 6.4g   Protein 20.7g

Fat 6.9g   Saturates 1.8g   Sugars 8.9g   Salt 0.62g

Fruit/Veg Portion 2

CHICKEN RECIPES

Turkey Burger

Servings: 8

Cooking Time: 15 Minutes

Ingredients:

- 1 slice wholemeal bread
- 1 egg, beaten
- 500g turkey breast mince
- 1 onion, finely grated
- 2 carrots, finely grated
- 4-6 cloves garlic, crushed
- pinch black pepper
- 8 wholemeal rolls, split (approx. 60g each)
- 150g lettuce
- 4 tomatoes, finely sliced
- 1 onion, finely sliced

Directions:

1. In a bowl, crumble the bread and add to the beaten egg. Set aside, but mix occasionally, until the bread has absorbed all the egg.

2. Add the turkey mince, onion, carrot, garlic and pepper to the egg and bread then mix well.

3. Form into 8 burgers (approx 8cm diameter and 2½cm thick) and put on a plate or tray, cover with cling film and place in the fridge for at least 20 minutes, but an hour or two is better.

4. Grill the burgers for 6-8 minutes on each side, ensuring they are fully cooked.

5. Toast the buns, if desired, and build your burgers with the lettuce, tomato and onion.

Recipe Tips

Spice up your burgers with a pinch of chilli flakes or 1 tsp ground cumin. Or add herbs such as thyme or rosemary.

For a festive zest, add 1 tbsp dried cranberries to the burger mix.

Freezing instructions: Can be frozen raw or cooked. Freeze in individually wrapped portions with greaseproof paper between each burger. Defrost fully in the fridge or microwave and heat thoroughly until piping-hot and cooked right through.

Nutrition:

KCal 297   Carbs 34.1g   Fibre 6.0g   Protein 28.7g

Fat 3.8g   Saturates 1.0g   Sugars 6.6g   Salt 0.8g

Fruit/Veg Portion 1

Turkey And Mushroom Mince

Servings: 6

Cooking Time: 15 Minutes

Ingredients:

- 1 tsp sunflower oil
- 3 onions, finely chopped
- 3 carrots, finely diced
- 500g turkey thigh mince
- 250g mushrooms, sliced
- 1 stick celery, finely diced
- 1 heaped tbsp plain flour
- 1 low-salt chicken stock cube dissolved in 500ml boiling water
- good pinch white pepper
- 2 tsp reduced-salt soy sauce

Directions:

1. Heat the oil in a pan. Add the onions and carrots and cook 4-5 minutes until the onions start to brown.

2. Add the turkey mince, mushrooms and celery. Cook for 4-5 minutes, breaking up any clumps of mince with a wooden spoon.

3. Sprinkle over the flour and mix well so that everything is coated. Gradually pour in the stock stirring continuously until it starts to thicken.

4. Add the pepper and soy sauce, stir and reduce the heat to low. Cover and simmer gently for 3-4 minutes.

Recipe Tips

Ideal served with leafy green vegetables and baked sweet potatoes.

This works well with pork, beef or lamb mince.

For a vegan version use a vegan alternative in place of mince and a vegetable stock cube.

To make a low-fat pie, put the mince in a pie dish and top with 4 sheets of filo pastry lightly brushed with 2 tsp rapeseed oil and bake for 7-10 minutes.

Freezing instructions: Suitable for freezing once cooked. Defrost in the fridge or microwave and reheat thoroughly until piping hot throughout.

Nutrition:

KCal 223   Carbs 11.6g   Fibre 4.2g   Protein 28.2g

Fat 7.2g   Saturates 2.1g   Sugars 7.8g   Salt 0.64g

Fruit/Veg Portion 2

Turkey And Chickpea Curry

Servings: 2

Cooking Time: 20 Minutes

Ingredients:

- 1 tsp oil
- 1 onion, sliced
- 1 tbsp medium curry paste
- 300ml chicken stock
- 200g cooked turkey, chopped
- 400g tin chickpeas, drained and rinsed
- 2 tomatoes, chopped
- 2 tbsp Greek yogurt
- coriander, to garnish

Directions:

1. Heat the oil in a non-stick pan. Add the onion and

fry for 2–3 minutes until softened.

2. Add the curry paste and continue to cook for 1 minute.

3. Add the stock, turkey, chickpeas and tomatoes, and simmer uncovered for 15 minutes.

4. Stir through the yogurt.

5. Serve with steamed rice and garnish with coriander.

Recipe Tips

Try wrapping the curry in chapattis or roti with salad. For extra vegetables, add a chopped red pepper along with the onions.

Nutrition:

KCal 447   Carbs 30.1g   Fibre 10.0g   Protein 42.7g

Fat 15.1g   Saturates 3.1g   Sugars 8.8g   Salt 0.07g

Fruit/Veg Portion 2

Turkey And Cranberry Pinwheel Tortillas

Servings: 12

Cooking Time: 3-4 Minutes

Ingredients:

- 4 wholemeal tortillas (approx. 65g each)
- 110g sliced cooked turkey
- 75g low-fat quark
- leaves 4 stems fresh thyme
- good grind black pepper
- 25g dried cranberries
- 4 Little Gem lettuce leaves, halved lengthways
- 4 thin spring onions, trimmed
- half red pepper, sliced in thin strips
- cocktail sticks

Directions:

1. Stack the tortillas on top of each other and trim the rounded edges off to create square tortillas.

2. Warm the trimmed tortillas in a dry frying pan, shuffling them so each gets exposed to the hot pan for 1 minute.

3. Lay the tortillas out on a work surface.

4. Leaving a 2cm border at the top of each tortilla, first arrange turkey slices over each square, then spread with the low-fat quark and sprinkle with the thyme, black pepper and cranberries. Keeping the top margin, get the filling right to the edges and bottom of each tortilla square. It doesn't matter if filling sticks out at the sides, you can trim it once rolled.

5. Lay the lettuce from left to right along the bottom edge of each tortilla. Above the lettuce lay a line of red pepper slices, and then – above that – place a spring onion.

6. Roll up tightly from the bottom, then with the seam on top secure each tortilla with 8 cocktail sticks.

7. With a sharp knife cut between the cocktail sticks to create 8 pinwheels, then arrange on a platter.

Nutrition:

KCal 90   Carbs 11.8g   Fibre 1.9g   Protein 6.1g   Fat 1.6g   Saturates 0.7g   Sugars 2.7g   Salt 0.24g

Fruit/Veg Portion 0

Tortillas Stuffed With Chicken And Salad

Servings: 2

Cooking Time: 10 Minutes

Ingredients:

- 1 tsp olive oil
- 1 small onion, chopped
- 1 red pepper, sliced
- 1 boneless, skinless, chicken breast, sliced (150g)
- 1 x 400g tin red kidney beans, drained and rinsed
- 1 tbsp half-fat crème fraiche
- 2 small flour tortillas
- 1 carrot, peeled and grated
- 60g mixed salad leaves
- freshly ground black pepper

Directions:

1. Heat the oil in a non-stick frying pan. Add the onion and red pepper and fry for 2-3 minutes, until softened. Add the chicken and fry for 3-4 minutes until browned and cooked through.
2. Meanwhile, in a bowl, mash together the kidney beans and crème fraiche. Warm the tortillas.
3. Divide the bean mixture between the tortillas and spoon over the chicken mixture. Add the carrot and salad leaves, season well, roll up and serve.

Recipe Tips

You could use sliced turkey escalopes in place of chicken. For a veggie version, replace the chicken with 200g sliced mushrooms.

Tortillas freeze well so you can freeze the pack and use as needed.

Nutrition:

KCal 484   Carbs 60.5g   Fibre 17.5g   Protein 33.7g

Fat 8.0g   Saturates 2.9g   Sugars 11.7g   Salt 1.1g

Fruit/Veg Portion 3

Thai Chicken Stir Fry

Servings: 2

Cooking Time: 10 Minutes

Ingredients:

- 1 tsp sunflower/rapeseed oil
- 2 boneless, skinless chicken breast, thinly sliced
- 2 cloves garlic, sliced
- 2.5cm fresh ginger, peeled and grated
- 1 red chilli, finely sliced
- 1 bunch spring onions, sliced
- 1 red pepper, seeded and cubed
- zest and juice 1 lime
- large bunch basil
- 1 tbsp reduced-salt soy sauce

Directions:

1. Heat the oil in a frying pan or wok, until it begins to smoke. Add the chicken and fry for 2–3 minutes until golden, remove from the pan with a slotted spoon and set aside.
2. Add the garlic, ginger and chilli and fry for 1 minute, add the spring onions and pepper and continue to fry for 2 minutes.

3. Return the chicken to the pan with the remaining ingredients and heat through, until piping hot. Serve.

Recipe Tips

This recipe also works well with thinly sliced lean pork or beef, prawns, salmon, turkey or tofu instead of chicken.

Great wrapped up in a tortilla or roti with salad.

If you don't have all the veggies to hand, you could use packets of stir fry veg, tinned bamboo shoots in water or sliced carrots.

Nutrition:

KCal 234   Carbs 10.0g   Fibre 3.0g   Protein 38.9g
Fat 3.6g   Saturates 0.6g   Sugars 7.5g   Salt 0.92g
Fruit/Veg Portion 1

Tandoori Chicken And Vegetables

Servings: 2

Cooking Time: 15 Minutes

Ingredients:

- 300g skinless chicken breast
- 1 tbsp low-fat natural yogurt
- 1 tsp paprika
- 1 tsp ground cumin
- 1 tsp turmeric
- 4 tomatoes, halved
- 1 tsp garam masala
- 1 tsp rapeseed oil
- 2 large red onions, quartered
- 1 red pepper, cut into 8 pieces

Directions:

1. Preheat the oven to 200°C/ gas 6. Cube the chicken and add to a bowl with the yogurt, paprika, cumin and turmeric, then mix well to coat the chicken.

2. Sprinkle the tomatoes with garam masala.

3. Lightly oil a baking tray and arrange the onion and pepper evenly over it, then place the chicken pieces on the onion and pepper, and arrange the tomatoes on top.

4. Roast for 15 minutes, or until the chicken is thoroughly cooked, and serve with basmati rice or salad.

Recipe Tips

Use curry paste if you don't have all the spices, or add grated fresh ginger and crushed garlic for extra flavour.

You can mix the chicken, spices and yogurt together in a food bag and keep in the fridge for a few hours before you start cooking, which helps the flavours to infuse.

Spicy dishes do not usually need any added salt, which means they're better for your heart.

Skinless chicken is rich in protein and has almost half the fat and saturated fat of skin-on chicken.

Freezing instructions: Suitable for freezing once cooked. Defrost in the fridge or microwave and reheat thoroughly until piping-hot throughout.

Nutrition:

KCal 318   Carbs 24.3g   Fibre 8.2g   Protein 40.6g
Fat 4.6g   Saturates 0.7g   Sugars 19.9g   Salt 0.28g
Fruit/Veg Portion 5

Tandoori Chicken Chapatti

Servings: 2

Cooking Time: 3 Minutes

Ingredients:

- half red pepper, thinly sliced
- half red onion, thinly sliced
- handful fresh coriander, roughly chopped
- juice half lime
- 1 tbsp fat-free Greek yogurt
- 1 tsp tandoori paste
- 100g cold, cooked chicken, chopped
- 2 chapattis (approx. 60g each)
- 2 handfuls mixed salad leaves

Directions:

1. Add the sliced red pepper, red onion, coriander and lime juice to a bowl. Mix well and reserve.
2. Meanwhile, in another bowl, mix the yogurt with the tandoori paste and then stir in the chopped chicken.
3. Place the chapattis in a preheated dry frying pan over a medium heat for 45 seconds on each side to warm them through.
4. Lay the chapattis out and spread the chicken over half of each chapatti. Add the salad leaves, then top with the red pepper and onion mixture.
5. Roll them up, tucking in the sides and enjoy.

Recipe Tips

The mix of yogurt and tandoori paste in this recipe gives you the moisture of mayonnaise without the fat. Try it mixed into cooked potatoes for a spicy potato salad.

Choose chapattis without fat and don't add extra fat when serving, if you're watching your weight.

Chapattis are made with wholemeal flour so are higher in fibre and great for making a quick meal. You could fill them with salad and avocado, or use leftover lamb instead of chicken.

Nutrition:

KCal 311 Carbs 31.9g Fibre 1.9g Protein 22.2g Fat 10.1g Saturates 0.5g Sugars 4.8g Salt 0.64g Fruit/Veg Portion 1

Szechuan Chicken

Servings: 3

Cooking Time: 8 Minutes

Ingredients:

- 1 tsp Szechuan/Sichuan pepper
- juice half lemon
- 2 tsp rapeseed oil
- 350g chicken breast, cut into strips
- 1 small red chilli, sliced into rings
- 4cm fresh ginger, finely chopped
- 2 garlic cloves, sliced
- 3 spring onions, cut into pieces
- 1 heaped tsp Chinese five-spice powder
- 20g sesame seeds
- 1 tbsp tomato puree

Directions:

1. Add the pepper to a cup with the lemon juice and set aside.
2. Heat the oil in a wok or frying pan and add the

chicken, stir constantly, for 3-4 minutes lightly browning the outside.

3. Add the chili, ginger and garlic and mix well for 2 Minutes

4. Add the spring onion, five-spice powder, sesame seeds and tomato puree. Mix well and cook for a further 2 minutes. Add 1-2tbsp water, remove from the heat and mix so the chicken gets coated.

5. Place in a serving dish and sprinkle with the pepper and lemon juice mixture.

Recipe Tips

Works well with strips of turkey, beef or pork or use prawns or chunks of salmon.

For a vegan version, use tofu in place of chicken.

Freezing instructions: Suitable for freezing once cooked. Defrost in the fridge or microwave and reheat thoroughly until piping hot throughout.

Nutrition:

KCal 198   Carbs 2.5g   Fibre 1.4g   Protein 30.1g   Fat 7.2g   Saturates 1.2g   Sugars 1.8g   Salt 0.19g Fruit/Veg Portion 0

Sweet And Sour Meatballs With Veggie Rice

Servings: 2

Cooking Time: 35 Minutes

Ingredients:

- 75g turkey breast mince
- half small onion, finely chopped
- 4 ready-to-eat dried apricots, finely chopped
- half tbsp fresh parsley, chopped
- 1 tbsp fresh breadcrumbs
- a little beaten egg
- For the rice:
- 100g basmati rice
- 1 tbsp frozen sweetcorn
- 1 tbsp frozen peas
- half small red or orange pepper, chopped
- For the sauce:
- 1 tsp rapeseed oil
- half small onion, finely chopped
- half small red or orange pepper, chopped
- 200g tin chopped tomatoes
- 1 tsp red wine vinegar

Directions:

1. Preheat the oven to 200ºC/ gas 6. Mix together the mince, onion, apricots, parsley and breadcrumbs in a bowl. Add enough egg to bind, and roll the mixture into 6–8 balls. (Let the kids help make the meatballs.) Place on a baking sheet and cook for 10–12 minutes.

2. Meanwhile, cook the basmati rice according to its pack instructions, adding the sweetcorn, peas and pepper 5 minutes before the end of its cooking time.

3. To make the sauce, heat the oil in a small pan and add the onion and pepper. Fry for 3 minutes.

4. Add the tomatoes and wine vinegar. Simmer for 1 minute.

5. Remove the mixture from the pan and pour into a blender and blend until smooth.

6. Return the mixture to the pan and add the cooked meatballs.

7. Heat through for 1 minute. Serve the meatballs and sauce on the rice.

Recipe Tips

Meatballs freeze well, so it's a good idea to make a batch to freeze. You could also make extra sauce and freeze individual portions of meatballs and sauce in plastic cups.

Freezing instructions: Freeze the sauce and meatballs separately. Defrost in the fridge or microwave and thoroughly reheat until piping-hot throughout.

Nutrition:

KCal 351   Carbs 57.8g   Fibre 4.3g   Protein 20.3g
Fat 3.3g   Saturates 0.5g   Sugars 10.8g   Salt 0.19g
Fruit/Veg Portion 2

Southern Style Chicken

Servings: 4

Cooking Time: 20 Minutes

Ingredients:

- 1 heaped tsp dried thyme
- 1 heaped tsp allspice
- 1 heaped tsp paprika
- 1 heaped tsp turmeric
- 1 heaped tsp oregano
- 1 tsp sage
- good grind black pepper
- 1 slice wholemeal bread, crumbled into 30g fine breadcrumbs
- 1 egg, beaten
- 450g chicken thighs, skin removed
- 1 tbsp plain flour
- 1 tsp rapeseed oil

Directions:

1. Preheat the oven to 180°C/gas 4. Mix all the spices and herbs together with the breadcrumbs, making sure they are well combined.

2. Beat the egg in a bowl and set aside.

3. Dredge the chicken with the flour, shaking off any excess and dip each chicken thigh into the beaten egg.

4. Toss the chicken pieces in the spicy breadcrumb mixture ensuring each thigh is thoroughly coated.

5. Lay the chicken on a lightly oiled baking sheet and sprinkle any leftover spice mixture on top.

6. Roast for 10 minutes, turn the pieces over and roast

for another 10 minutes. Check the chicken is cooked through and serve.

Recipe Tips

You could use chicken breasts or turkey escalopes with this coating.

When coating the chicken use just one hand and keep the other clean, otherwise you can get into a sticky mess! You could add other spices. For a spicy kick try cayenne pepper, or give it a Chinese flavour with a pinch of Chinese five-spice.

Nutrition:

KCal 193   Carbs 6.6g   Fibre 2.1g   Protein 27.1g   Fat 6.0g   Saturates 1.5g   Sugars 0.4g   Salt 0.39g   Fruit/Veg Portion 0

Smoky Chicken Kebabs

Servings: 8

Cooking Time: 10 Minutes

Ingredients:

- For the marinade:
- 2 tbsp toasted coriander seeds
- 1 tbsp toasted cumin seeds
- 4 cloves garlic, peeled
- 4cm piece ginger, roughly chopped
- 2 red chillies, deseeded and roughly chopped
- freshly ground black pepper
- 1 tbsp sun-dried tomato purée
- 3 tbsp white wine vinegar
- 3 tbsp extra-virgin olive oil
- For the kebabs:

- 8 small chicken breasts (approx.1kg), cut into 2.5-3.5cm cubes
- 4 medium courgettes, cut into 2cm thick rings
- 8 lemon/lime wedges, to serve

Directions:

1. To make the marinade, grind the coriander and cumin seeds to a powder.

2. Pound the garlic, ginger and chillies with a pinch of pepper, to a rough paste in a mortar.

3. Work in the coriander and cumin, tomato purée, vinegar, and olive oil. Mix in 2 tbsp water. Pour over the chicken pieces, and turn to coat each one.

4. Leave for at least half an hour (or up to 24 hours, covered, in the fridge).

5. Preheat the grill or bbq thoroughly. Thread the chicken pieces onto 8 long skewers or 16 small ones, alternating with courgette rings. Grill or barbecue for around 10 minutes, turning several times until browned and cooked through. Serve with lemon or lime wedges, and rice or salad.

Recipe Tips

If you don't have a pestle and mortar, simply blend the marinade ingredients with a stick blender or food processor.

You could use cubes of salmon instead of chicken or tofu cubes for a vegan version.

Nutrition:

KCal 205   Carbs 1.9g   Fibre 2.9g   Protein 32.4g   Fat 6.9g   Saturates 1.1g   Sugars 1.6g   Salt 0.2g   Fruit/Veg Portion 0

Roast Turkey

Servings: 10

Cooking Time: 3 Hours

Ingredients:

- 5kg turkey, fresh or thoroughly defrosted
- 1 lemon, quartered
- 1 onion, unpeeled and quartered
- 2-3 whole garlic cloves, unpeeled and crushed lightly
- 2 bay leaves
- Good sprig of fresh thyme
- 12 thin rashers of streaky bacon

Directions:

1. Preheat the oven to 220°C/gas 8. Cook your turkey at this temperature for the first 30 mins and then lower the oven temperature to 190°C/gas 5.
2. Stuff the turkey's cavity with the lemon, onion quarters, garlic, bay leaves and thyme.
3. Put the turkey into a large roasting tin. Lay the bacon across the turkey breast (see chefs tips), then cover it with foil.
4. Cook for at least 3 hours, removing the foil for the last 30 minutes of cooking time so that the bacon and skin can brown.
5. Check the turkey is cooked, then remove from the oven, cover loosely with the foil and leave to one side to rest for 30 minutes before carving.

Recipe Tips

Different sized turkeys will require different cooking times. The cooking time will be approximately 30-35 mins per kg.

Your turkey should be moist and succulent. It's ready when the juices run clear. Test by plunging a fork into the deepest part of the thigh or breast. If using a thermometer, the internal cooked temperature will be 165°F/74°C.

To make a bacon weave: simply interweave the rashers of bacon on a piece of cling film, once you have a neat weave carefully place it on the turkey breast and remove the film.

Nutrition:

KCal 243   Carbs 0.0g   Fibre 0.0g   Protein 36.1g   Fat 10.9g   Saturates 3.8g   Sugars 0.5g   Salt 1.23g   Fruit/Veg Portion 0

Roast Chicken

Servings: 8

Cooking Time: 1 Hour and 50 Minutes

Ingredients:

- 2kg whole chicken
- 1 lemon, halved
- good handful fresh herbs (rosemary and thyme are ideal)
- freshly ground black pepper
- 300ml boiling water

Directions:

1. Preheat the oven to 180°C/gas mark 4.
2. Place the chicken onto a rack and place over a roasting tin. Squeeze the lemon over the bird and place the lemon shells in the cavity of the bird.

3. Place some of the herbs on top of the bird and place the remaining herbs into the cavity. Season with black pepper.

4. Pour the water into the roasting tin, then place in the oven and cook for 45 minutes per kilo, plus 20 minutes (1 hour and 50 minutes for a 2kg bird), topping up the water if necessary.

5. Take out of the oven, cover with foil and allow to stand for 15 minutes.

6. Remove the skin, carve, and serve with plenty of vegetables and potatoes.

Recipe Tips

To check if the chicken is cooked, pierce the skin between the thigh and breast – the juices should be clear. If using the pan juices to make gravy, pour into a jug and allow to stand for a few minutes. The fat will float to the top and can be removed with a spoon before making the gravy.

Freezing instructions: Suitable for freezing once cooked. For convinience, you can freeze this dish in portions, then defrost in the fridge or microwave and reheat thoroughly until piping hot throughout.

Nutrition:

KCal 209   Carbs 0.3g   Fibre 0.4g   Protein 37.1g   Fat 6.5g   Saturates 1.8g   Sugars 0.2g   Salt 0.33g Fruit/Veg Portion 0

Quick Chicken Korma

Servings: 2

Cooking Time: 20 Minutes

Ingredients:

- 1 tsp rapeseed oil
- 1 onion, chopped
- 2 tbsp korma curry paste
- 1 x 200g can chopped tomatoes
- 2 medium chicken breasts, chopped
- 1 tbsp ground almonds
- 150g carton natural low-fat yogurt
- 1 tsp toasted flaked almonds, to garnish
- basmati rice, to serve

Directions:

1. Heat the oil in a non-stick frying pan.

2. Add the onion and fry for 4-5 minutes until softened. Add the curry paste and continue to fry for 2 minutes.

3. Add the tomatoes, bring to the boil and simmer for 2 minutes.

4. Transfer to a food processor and blend until almost smooth.

5. Return to the pan, add the chicken and heat for 5-7 minutes or until the chicken is cooked.

6. Stir in the ground almonds and yogurt, heat through gently - without boiling. Top with a few toasted almonds and serve with plenty of steamed basmati rice.

Recipe Tips

This is also great served cold with plenty of salad in a

rolled-up roti or tortilla.

For a veggie version, just make the sauce then toss in chunks of cooked sweet potatoes and sautéed whole mushrooms in place of the chicken.

Freezing instructions: Suitable for freezing once cooked. Then defrost in the fridge or microwave and reheat thoroughly until piping hot throughout.

Nutrition:

KCal 363   Carbs 17.8g   Fibre 3.4g   Protein 44.4g   Fat 12.0g   Saturates 1.9g   Sugars 15.2g   Salt 1.08g   Fruit/Veg Portion 2

Piri Piri Chicken

Servings: 2

Cooking Time: 6-8 Minutes

Ingredients:

- 2 skinless chicken breasts (approx. 350g)
- 2 tsp olive oil
- 1–2 red chillies, finely chopped
- 4 cloves garlic, crushed
- 2 tsp paprika
- juice 1 lime
- 1 lime, to serve

Directions:

1. Slice the chicken breasts into 2-3 pieces, depending on size, to create 1cm thick slices.

2. Place the chicken slices in a food bag and add the olive oil, chillies, garlic, paprika and lime juice. Mix well so the chicken is coated. Set aside for 15 minutes or place in the fridge and leave overnight.

3. Heat your grill, barbecue or griddle pan and add the chicken. Turn over after 3 minutes and cook for another 3 minutes. Check it's cooked through, ensuring there is no pink meat in the middle. Place on a plate.

4. Finally, cut the lime in half and pop it, cut-side down, onto the griddle for a couple of minutes. Serve with the chicken.

Recipe Tips

You could also use this piri piri marinade on turkey or pork escalopes, too.

For a veggie version, cook and cool large chunks of vegetables such as carrots, beetroot, sweet potatoes, potatoes or butternut squash and marinate them in the piri piri mixture before grilling or barbecuing.

To freeze, wrap in foil/greaseproof inside freezer bags and label. They'll keep for up to 3 months.

Nutrition:

KCal 229   Carbs 1.3g   Fibre 1.4g   Protein 43.1g   Fat 5.4g   Saturates 1.0g   Sugars 0.8g   Salt 0.27g   Fruit/Veg Portion 0

Pho

Servings: 4

Cooking Time: 35 Minutes

Ingredients:

- 2 tsp rapeseed oil
- 1 onion, finely chopped
- 5cm fresh ginger, finely chopped
- 4 cloves garlic, thinly sliced
- 2 star anise
- 5cm stick cinnamon
- half tsp coriander seeds
- 1 bird's eye chilli, split and 4 to garnish
- 1 chicken breast, boneless and skinless
- 1 reduced-salt chicken stock cube in 600ml boiling water
- 1 head of broccoli, broken into florets
- 1 carrot, cut into ribbons with a vegetable peeler
- 300g precooked rice noodles
- 300g beansprouts
- 1 bunch spring onion, sliced
- 30g fresh coriander, roughly chopped
- 1 lime to serve

Directions:

1. Add the oil to a pan with the onion and cook for 4-5 minutes. Stir regularly until well browned.
2. Add the ginger and garlic, and cook for a further 2-3 minutes.
3. Add the star anise, cinnamon, coriander seeds, chilli and the chicken breast. Mix well and cook for 3-4 minutes, ensuring the chicken breast is lightly browned and coated with the spices.
4. Add the stock and mix well again. Bring to the boil, then turn down the heat. Cover, then simmer gently for 15 minutes.
5. Remove the chilli, cinnamon stick and star anise and discard. Remove the chicken breast and set to one side.
6. Add the broccoli and cook for 5 minutes, then add the carrot and cook a further 2 minutes before adding the noodles and beansprouts. Bring to the boil, then divide between 4 bowls.
7. Slice the chicken and place some on top of each bowl, then scatter with spring onion, coriander, a chilli and a squeeze of fresh lime.

Recipe Tips

You could add pork instead of chicken, or add prawns with the broccoli.

For a vegan version, replace the chicken with tofu and use a vegetable stock cube.

For gluten-free version, use a gluten-free stock cube.

Nutrition:

KCal 241   Carbs 30.6g   Fibre 7.3g   Protein 17.0g

Fat 4.0g   Saturates 0.5g   Sugars 10.5g   Salt 0.25g

Fruit/Veg Portion 2

FISH & SEAFOOD RECIPES

Sweet Potato Crab Cakes With Green Chilli Dip

Servings: 25

Cooking Time: 25 Minutes

Ingredients:

- 200g sweet potato, boiled and mashed
- 1 tbsp flour (plus a little for dusting)
- 1 egg, beaten
- good pinch pepper
- 20g fresh dill, chopped
- 3 spring onions, finely chopped
- 200g cooked crab meat, dark and brown
- grated zest 1 lemon (plus wedges to serve)
- 2 tsp rapeseed oil
- For the salsa:
- 2 tomatoes, roughly chopped
- 1 heaped tbsp tomato puree
- 1 green chilli, de-seeded and very finely chopped

Directions:

1. Prepare the potatoes and allow to cool.
2. Add the flour, egg, pepper and dill to the mashed potato and mix well.
3. Stir in the spring onion and crab, combine together then form into small patties approx. 1 cm deep, then dust with flour.
4. Add 1 tsp oil to a non-stick pan, fry for 1-2 minutes turning carefully a couple of times to ensure even cooking (about 6 minutes altogether) until lightly golden and firm, making sure the patties are cooked through.
5. Meanwhile, for the salsa, blend the tomatoes with the tomato puree and stir in the green chilli.

Recipe Tips

For flavour, the mixture of white and dark crab is ideal. Try making with salmon and/ or chopped prawns.

Nutrition:

KCal 27   Carbs 2.6g   Fibre 0.4g   Protein 2.2g   Fat 0.8g   Saturates 0.1g   Sugars 0.8g   Salt 0.09g Fruit/Veg Portion 0

Squid And Prawn Skewers

Servings: 10

Cooking Time: 5 Minutes

Ingredients:

- 300g raw squid rings
- 165g raw peeled jumbo king prawns
- 1 clove garlic, crushed
- 1 small red chilli, finely chopped
- juice and finely grated zest 1 lemon
- 1 tsp rapeseed oil

Directions:

1. Mix the squid and prawns with the garlic, chilli, lemon juice and zest, saving a little zest to garnish.

Leave to marinate for 5 mins.

2. Thread a squid ring, a prawn and another squid ring onto each skewer.

3. Heat the oil in a large, non-stick frying pan and cook the skewers, turning once, to ensure the prawns are fully cooked.

Recipe Tips

If using wooden skewers, soak them in water for 10 minutes before threading on the seafood.

The skewers can also be cooked under a hot grill for 4-5 minutes turning once, to ensure the prawn is fully cooked through. Put a little foil over the exposed wood on the skewers to prevent them from burning under the grill.

Nutrition:

KCal 42   Carbs 0.1g   Fibre 0.0g   Protein 7.6g   Fat 1.1g   Saturates 0.2g   Sugars 0.1g   Salt 0.17g Fruit/Veg Portion 0

Spicy Prawn And Pak Choi Stir-Fry

Servings: 2

Cooking Time: 10 Minutes

Ingredients:

- 1 onion, thinly sliced
- 1 red pepper, thinly sliced
- 4 chestnut mushrooms, sliced
- 2 cloves garlic, crushed
- half red chilli, chopped (or pinch chilli flakes)
- 1 tbsp rapeseed oil
- 150g raw king prawns
- 2 tsp reduced-salt soy sauce
- 1 heaped tsp Chinese five-spice
- 2 pak choi, leaves left whole and stems chopped
- 2 tbsp water

Directions:

1. Prepare the onion, red pepper, chestnut mushrooms, garlic and red chilli, and set aside.

2. Heat a wok or large frying pan over a high heat, add the rapeseed oil and when hot add the onion. Stir-fry for 2 minutes, then add the red pepper, mushrooms, garlic and chilli, and stir-fry for 1 minute.

3. Add the prawns, soy sauce, Chinese five-spice and pak choi stems, and keep stirring for a further 3–4 minutes until the prawns are cooked. The flesh of the prawns should turn pink or orange when cooked and loose their translucent appearance.

4. Add the pak choi leaves and water, cover with a lid and cook for a further minute. Mix well and serve immediately.

5. Serve with noodles or a few thin slices of red chilli and a wedge of lime.

Recipe Tips

Assemble the ingredients first, ready to throw into the pan. And, always make sure the pan is really hot before you start adding them.

Stir-frying is a quick way to cook and more nutrients are retained in your food. You don't need much oil and as long as you keep stirring it around the pan, the food is steamed rather than fried.

Nutrition:

KCal 184   Carbs 11.4g   Fibre 5.7g   Protein 17.4g   Fat 6.5g   Saturates 0.6g   Sugars 9.1g   Salt 0.85g   Fruit/Veg Portion 3

Spicy Crab Tortilla

Servings: 4

Cooking Time: 15 Minutes

Ingredients:

- 1 tsp rapeseed oil
- 1 onion, finely chopped
- 2.5cm fresh ginger, peeled and grated
- 1 clove garlic, crushed
- 1 tsp dried red chilli flakes
- 1 tsp ground cumin
- 240g cooked white crab meat
- 3 tbsp fresh coriander, chopped
- 8 small flour tortillas (approx. 40g each)
- 100g mixed salad leaves
- 4 medium tomatoes, sliced
- 8 lime wedges, to serve

Directions:

1. Heat the oil in non-stick frying pan. Add the onion, ginger, garlic, chilli flakes and cumin and fry for 2–3 minutes.

2. Remove the pan from the heat and stir in the crab meat and coriander.

3. Warm the tortilla according to the pack insructions.

4. Add some salad leaves and tomato slices to each tortilla. Top with the crab mixture and a squeeze of lime.

Recipe Tips

To warm tortillas, add them all in a stack to a dry frying pan over a medium heat, take the bottom one and move to the top and keep doing this until they have all had a minute in contact with the hot pan. You can repeat on the other side for 30 seconds to get them really hot but still keep them soft and pliable.

Nutrition:

KCal 336   Carbs 47.4g   Fibre 4.7g   Protein 19.7g   Fat 6.5g   Saturates 2.4g   Sugars 6.6g   Salt 1.49g   Fruit/Veg Portion 1

Speedy Salmon Pasta

Servings: 2

Cooking Time: 10 Minutes

Ingredients:

- 2 tbsp mixed fresh herbs, chopped (e.g. parsley, coriander)
- grated zest and juice 1 lime
- 2 pieces skinless, salmon fillet (approx. 100g each)
- 150g pasta shapes
- 100g sugarsnap peas
- 2 tomatoes, chopped

Directions:

1. Mix together the herbs and lime rind and juice in a non-metallic bowl. Add the salmon and set aside to marinate for at least 10 minutes.

2. Meanwhile, cook the pasta according to the pack

temperature and stop the rice cooking. Add a little at a time; if you run out just add a little boiling water.

Stirring regularly, with a wooden spoon, means rice releases its starch and ensures a creamy texture.

Nutrition:

KCal 374   Carbs 49.4g   Fibre 3.2g   Protein 21.4g   Fat 9.4g   Saturates 1.6g   Sugars 6.8g   Salt 0.78g   Fruit/Veg Portion 1

Seafood Parcels

Servings: 2

Cooking Time: 20 Minutes

Ingredients:

- 160g broccoli florets
- 100g salmon, cubed
- 100g pollock, cut into 2 chunks
- 50g prawns
- 6 spring onions, sliced
- 1 red pepper, cut into strips
- 10g parsley
- black pepper
- juice lemon, plus 2 wedges to serve
- 2 tbsp water
- 2 tsp olive oil

Directions:

1. Preheat the oven to 180°C/gas 5. Blanch the broccoli for 3–4 minutes in boiling water and drain.
2. Divide the fish, seafood and vegetables equally between 2 large squares of foil measuring 25cm x 25cm.
3. Sprinkle with the parsley and a good grind of pepper. Squeeze lemon over each, and then add the water and olive oil.
4. Fold the foil into the centre to make a parcel, then place on a baking sheet and bake for 15 minutes.
5. Serve each parcel with a lemon wedge.

Recipe Tips

This dish works with any white fish. Alternatively, you could just add salmon, or omit prawns.

Nutrition:

KCal 257   Carbs 7.9g   Fibre 5.9g   Protein 27.2g   Fat 11.7g   Saturates 2.1g   Sugars 6.8g   Salt 0.31g   Fruit/Veg Portion 2

Scandinavian Pickled Cucumber And Salad Sandwich

Servings: 4

Ingredients:

- 175g cucumber, very thinly sliced
- 1 red onion, very thinly sliced
- juice half lemon
- 2 tsp horseradish sauce
- 2 tsp mayonnaise
- 2 tbsp low-fat natural yogurt
- 4 slices (approx. 25g per slice) German-style dark wholegrain rye bread
- 4 handfuls mixed salad leaves
- 100g smoked salmon
- 1 tsp small capers
- black pepper

- 4 wedges lemon, to serve

Directions:

1. Mix the cucumber, red onion and lemon juice together and set aside.

2. Mix the horseradish, mayonnaise and yogurt in a small bowl or cup.

3. Spread each slice of rye bread with 1 tsp of the horseradish dressing.

4. Scatter the salad leaves over the bread, then scatter half the cucumber and onion over the salad and drizzle the rest of the sauce on top.

5. Now garnish with a little smoked salmon and scatter with the remaining onion and cucumber.

6. Add a few small capers, a good grind of fresh black pepper and lemon wedges to serve.

Recipe Tips

There are a lot of different types of rye bread available, but always look for wholegrain.

If you find the flavour a little strong, try a loaf made with sunflower or pumpkin seeds, instead.

Nutrition:

KCal 151   Carbs 15.9g   Fibre 1.8g   Protein 8.7g   Fat 5.5g   Saturates 1.0g   Sugars 6.0g   Salt 1.15g   Fruit/Veg Portion 1

Scallops With Lime And Chilli Butter

Servings: 4

Cooking Time: 5 Minutes

Ingredients:

- 15g butter, softened
- 1 tbsp olive oil
- half-1 red chilli, finely chopped
- grated rind and juice 1 lime
- freshly ground black pepper
- 12 scallops, cleaned
- rocket leaves, to serve

Directions:

1. In a small bowl, beat together the butter, oil, chilli and rind and juice of the lime. Season well.

2. Heat a non-stick frying pan, add the butter mixture and heat until bubbling. Add the scallops and fry for about 1 minute on each side.

3. Remove from the pan, serve with a little rocket and drizzle with the pan juices.

Recipe Tips

You could also add 2cm finely chopped fresh ginger and 2 cloves crushed garlic to the butter.

This recipe also works with prawns or cubes of fresh salmon.

Nutrition:

KCal 153   Carbs 0.1g   Fibre 0.4g   Protein 21.8g   Fat 7.2g   Saturates 2.7g   Sugars 0.1g   Salt 0.49g   Fruit/Veg Portion 0

Salmon, Red Onion And Sweet Pepper Wraps

Servings: 2

Cooking Time: 2 Minutes

Ingredients:

- 200g tin red salmon
- half red onion, finely chopped
- 1 red pepper, finely chopped
- 50g cucumber, finely diced
- 50g low-fat yogurt
- juice half lemon
- good grind black pepper
- 2 wholemeal tortillas, 70g each
- 50g salad leaves

Directions:

1. Drain the salmon and remove the skin, but keep the bones as they are packed with calcium. Add to a bowl and mash roughly with a fork.

2. Add the onion, red pepper, cucumber, yogurt, lemon juice and black pepper to the salmon and mix well.

3. Warm the tortillas in a dry frying pan or griddle pan for 1-2 minutes. Place on a clean work surface, divide the salad and the salmon between the two tortillas, placing the mixture in the middle and leaving a 3-4cm gap around the edges.

4. Roll up, tucking in the edges, then cut in half at an angle to serve.

Recipe Tips

For packed lunches or picnics, roll the packed tortilla tightly in greaseproof paper or foil, twisting the ends to secure. When eating just unwrap one end and peel the paper off as you eat it, tearing in a spiral as you munch your way down.

Try using tuna in place of salmon and spice it up with a little chili powder, or add herbs such as fresh coriander or dill.

Nutrition:

KCal 396   Carbs 39.0g   Fibre 6.0g   Protein 32.7g

Fat 10.8g   Saturates 3.0g   Sugars 9.0g   Salt 1.61g

Fruit/Veg Portion 1

Salmon PâtÉ

Servings: 2

Ingredients:

- 212g tin wild pacific pink salmon
- 4 spring onions, finely chopped
- 1tbsp capers, rinsed and roughly chopped
- half red pepper, finely chopped
- 5cm cucumber, deseeded and finely chopped
- 1 tbsp finely chopped fresh dill/parsley, plus sprig to serve
- juice half lemon
- good pinch white pepper
- 25g reduced-fat cream cheese

Directions:

1. Remove the skin from the salmon but retain the bones. Add to a bowl, then mix in all the ingredients, except the cream cheese, and mix well.

2. Stir in the cream cheese, mix again and serve topped with a sprig of dill.

3. Serve with small squares of toast.

Recipe Tips

'At risk' groups such as infants, children, pregnant women, the elderly and those who are unwell should avoid eating ready-to-eat, cold-smoked or cured fish. Therefore, this recipe is not suitable if this applies to you.

Ideal for spreading on toast, rolling into wraps or as a super sandwich.

Add a little 0% fat Greek yogurt to use as a party dip.

Spice it up with 1 tsp smoked paprika or chilli seasoning.

Nutrition:

KCal 209   Carbs 4.6g   Fibre 1.6g   Protein 27.3g   Fat 8.7g   Saturates 2.3g   Sugars 3.9g   Salt 1.55g

Salmon On Fennel Ratatouille

Servings: 1

Cooking Time: 15 Minutes

Ingredients:

- 1tsp olive oil
- 1 small red onion, roughly chopped
- 1 yellow pepper, chopped
- 1 clove garlic, crushed
- good pinch dried oregano
- pinch pepper
- 2 fresh ripe tomatoes, chopped
- half small head fennel, thinly sliced
- 1 125g salmon fillet
- 2 tbsp water
- fresh basil leaves, to serve

Directions:

1. Put the oil in a large pan on medium heat. Add the onion and stir for 2–3 minutes until it softens.

2. Now add the yellow pepper and stir regularly for 3–4 minutes.

3. Add the garlic, oregano, seasoning, tomatoes and fennel. Stir for 2 more minutes and bring to a simmer.

4. Place the salmon on top of the ratatouille, add the water and cover with a lid or with foil. Simmer gently for 4–5 minutes or until the salmon is cooked through.

5. Remove the salmon, stir a few torn fresh basil leaves into the ratatouille and serve.

Recipe Tips

Use sea bass or cod instead of salmon.

Add an aubergine to the ratatouille.

Nutrition:

KCal 421   Carbs 20.0g   Fibre 10.3g   Protein 29.3g   Fat 22.5g   Saturates 3.9g   Sugars 18.0g   Salt 0.18g   Fruit/Veg Portion 6

Salmon In Broccoli And Leek Sauce

Servings: 4

Cooking Time: 25 Minutes

Ingredients:

- 1 low-salt fish stock cube, dissolved in 200ml boiling water
- 320g broccoli, in florets
- 150g leeks, chopped
- 175ml semi-skimmed milk
- 1 tbsp cornflour, dissolved in 25ml semi-skimmed milk
- 1 tsp Dijon mustard
- good pinch white pepper
- 15g Parmesan cheese
- 400g salmon, cubed
- 1 tbsp reduced-fat cream cheese
- 10g fresh parsley, chopped

Directions:

1. Add the fish stock to a large pan.
2. Add the broccoli and the leeks. Simmer gently for 7–8 minutes, then stir the semi-skimmed milk and bring to a simmer.
3. Meanwhile, add the cornflour mixture to the pan, stirring until it starts to thicken.
4. Next, stir in the Dijon mustard, white pepper and Parmesan cheese. Add the salmon, cover and cook for 3–4 minutes, or until the fish is just cooked through.
5. Carefully stir in the cream cheese and chopped parsley. Finish the dish with a sprinkle of chopped parsley and serve.

Recipe Tips

This recipe would work well with most types of fish.

Nutrition:

KCal 332   Carbs 10.4g   Fibre 4.8g   Protein 28.5g
Fat 18.5g   Saturates 4.6g   Sugars 4.9g   Salt 0.44g
Fruit/Veg Portion 1

Salmon Fishcakes

Servings: 2

Cooking Time: 20 Minutes

Ingredients:

- 350g potatoes, peeled and chopped
- 300g fresh salmon, poached and flaked, or tinned if you prefer
- 2 spring onions, sliced
- 2 anchovy fillets, chopped
- handful fresh herbs, (e.g. parsley and dill), chopped
- 1 tbsp light mayonnaise
- black pepper, freshly ground
- flour, for dusting
- 1 egg, beaten
- 2 slices granary bread, in breadcrumbs
- 2 tsp vegetable oil
- lemon wedges, to serve

Directions:

1. Boil the potatoes 10-15 minutes until tender, then

mash.

2. Roughly mash together the salmon, potato, spring onion, anchovies, herbs and mayonnaise and season well

3. Form into 4 patties and chill for about 30 minutes.

4. Dust each fishcake in flour, then dip in the egg and coat in breadcrumbs.

5. Place the fishcakes on an oiled baking sheet and drizzle with a little oil.

6. Cook under a medium grill for 2–3 minutes on each side. Serve with lemon wedges.

Recipe Tips

Try using a mixture of fish such as salmon, crab and prawns.

You could use wholemeal bread to make a higher fibre, slightly denser fishcake.

Freezing instructions: Suitable for freezing once cooked. Freeze in individually wrapped portions with greaseproof paper between each fishcake. Defrost in the fridge, or in the microwave and heat thoroughly until piping-hot throughout.

Nutrition:

KCal 681   Carbs 54.4g   Fibre 5.9g   Protein 42.6g
Fat 31.3g   Saturates 5.7g   Sugars 4.1g   Salt 1.14g
Fruit/Veg Portion 0

Salmon And Spinach Filo Tarts

Servings: 4

Cooking Time: 25 Minutes

Ingredients:

- 1 tbsp vegetable oil
- 100g filo pastry
- 1 yellow pepper, chopped
- 4 spring onions, finely sliced
- 75g cooked and drained spinach (defrosted frozen is ideal)
- good pinch pepper
- 15g dill, roughly chopped but reserving 4 sprigs to garnish
- 2 boneless, skinless salmon steaks (approx. 125g each), cut into small cubes
- 1 egg, beaten with 100ml milk
- 8 cherry tomatoes, sliced
- lemon wedges, to garnish

Directions:

1. Preheat the oven to 180°C/gas 4. For the filo pastry, Lightly spray oil onto a large baking sheet, place on it 4 oven proof dishes (approx. 10cm across and 2 cm deep) upside down and spray with a little oil.

2. Divide the mixture between the pastry cases and add the salmon to each case and pour over the milk and egg mixture.

3. Arrange 3 filo squares, oiled side down, over each of the dishes to create a flower shape.

4. Carefully cover with a damp tea towel and set aside.

5. Lightly spray a little oil into a pan and add the

yellow pepper. Cook for 3-4 minutes until softened, and add the spring onions. Cook for a further minute, stir in the spinach, pepper and chopped dill.

6. Divide the mixture between the pastry cases and add the salmon to each case and pour over the milk and egg mixture.

7. Top with the tomato halves and use a scrunched offcut of pastry to make a shape in the centre.

8. Cook for 15 minutes. Serve topped with a sprig of dill and a wedge of lemon on the side.

Recipe Tips

Make sure you keep the filo pastry damp throughout. Cover it with a damp tea towel until you use it. Only make the filo cases just before you plan to fill them.

If you don't have small oven proof dishes you could make one large tart.

Nutrition:

KCal 267   Carbs 18.4g   Fibre 2.8g   Protein 18.9g

Fat 12.4g   Saturates 2.5g   Sugars 4.9g   Salt 0.39g

Fruit/Veg Portion 1

FRUIT RECIPES

Summer Berry Posset

Servings: 4

Ingredients:

- 100g raspberries
- 100g blueberries, saving 4 berries to top
- 2 tbsp reduced-sugar strawberry jam
- 300g low-fat natural yogurt
- 100g half-fat crème fraiche

Directions:

1. Add the raspberries and blueberries to the jam, mash with a fork and mix well.
2. Add half the berry mixture to the yogurt and crème fraiche, and mix well.
3. Divide the rest of the berry mixture between four glasses, placing a blob in the bottom of each and drizzling a little around the inside.
4. Divide the yogurt mixture between the glasses, topping each with a blueberry.

Recipe Tips

For a variation, try using fresh apricots and apricot jam, or add crunch with a sprinkle of toasted almonds or chopped hazelnuts.

Half-fat crème fraîche has less than a third of the fat of double cream and also contains more protein.

Berries contain antioxidants and vitamins – especially vitamin C. The pigments that give them their different colours contain phytonutrients and flavonoids. They are a good source of fibre.

Nutrition:

KCal 113 Carbs 12.3g Fibre 1.4g Protein 4.8g Fat 4.6g Saturates 3.1g Sugars 11.8g Salt 0.15g

Summer Berry Crush

Servings: 2

Ingredients:

- 200g frozen mixed summer berries, defrosted
- 200g carton virtually fat-free fromage frais
- Sugar free sweetener to taste
- 25g amaretti biscuits, lightly crushed

Directions:

1. Gently fold together all the ingredients and spoon into serving glasses.

Recipe Tips

If you don't have amaretti biscuits, you could use shortbread or ginger biscuits.

For a vegan version, use a soya-based yogurt in place of the fromage frais.

Nutrition:

KCal 137 Carbs 16.0g Fibre 3.1g Protein 10.1g Fat 3.0g Saturates 0.5g Sugars 9.9g Salt 0.1g Fruit/Veg Portion 1

Summerberry Smoothie

Servings: 1

Ingredients:

- 50g frozen raspberries
- 50g frozen strawberries
- 200ml skimmed milk
- sugar-free and calorie-free sweetener, to taste

Directions:

1. Place the berries and the milk in a food processor or blender and blend until smooth and frothy, sweeten to taste and serve.

Recipe Tips

Add 1 tbsp low-fat live yogurt to introduce some probiotics to your diet.

You could use other fruits such as mango, banana, peaches, nectarines or just one type of berry. If using very ripe fruits, you shouldn't need to add sweetener.

Summerberries are naturally lower in carbohydrate than tropical fruits such as banana or mango.

For a dairy alternative, swap to unsweetened, fortified plant-based milk.

Nutrition:

KCal 100 Carbs 14.4g Fibre 2.6g Protein 7.8g Fat 0.6g Saturates 0.2g Sugars 14.4g Salt 0.3g Fruit/Veg Portion 1

Stuffed Baked Apples

Servings: 6

Cooking Time: 35 Minutes

Ingredients:

- 20g walnuts
- 30g dried apricots
- 25g sultanas
- 1 tsp ground cinnamon
- 20g pumpkin seeds
- finely-grated zest and juice 1 orange
- 6 eating apples, unpeeled and cored)
- 1 tbsp water

Directions:

2. Preheat the oven to 180°C / gas 4
3. Mix together the walnuts, apricots and sultanas, then place on a board. Finely chop together to create a paste, then mix in the pumpkin seeds, cinnamon and orange zest.
4. Stuff the centre of each apple with the mixture, pressing it firmly into the fruit.
5. Place the apples into an ovenproof dish with the water, then drizzle the orange juice over them.
6. Cover with foil and bake for 20 minutes. Remove the foil and continue to bake for 10-15 minutes.
7. Serve with a dollop of low-fat yogurt or non-dairy alternative.

Recipe Tips

Experiment with different combinations of fruits and nuts for the filling.

Try with cranberries and mixed spice for a Christmas

flavour.

Nutrition:

KCal 122 Carbs 16.9g Fibre 2.4g Protein 2.6g Fat 4.3g Saturates 0.6g Sugars 16.4g Salt 0.01g Fruit/Veg Portion 1

Sticky Lemon Polenta Cake

Servings: 8

Cooking Time: 25 minutes + 20 mins cooling time

Ingredients:

- 2 tsp lemon extract
- juice and finely grated zest 1 lemon
- 3 tbsp granulated sweetener
- 2 eggs, beaten
- 50ml rapeseed oil (and 1 tsp to oil a 1lb loaf tin)
- 50ml water
- 100g instant polenta
- 1 tsp bicarbonate of soda
- For the drizzle:
- juice and finely grated zest 1 lemon
- 1 tbsp granulated sweetener
- 1 dessertspoon honey

Directions:

1. Preheat the oven to 180°/gas 4.

2. Oil the loaf tin and set aside ready to use.

3. In a bowl, add the lemon extract, juice and zest of 1 lemon, sweetener, eggs and oil then beat together well.

4. Stir in the water and beat again until frothy, gently stir in the polenta and bicarbonate of soda then immediately place in the baking tin and bake for 20-25 minutes.

5. Remove the cake from the oven and allow to cool for 20 minutes.

6. Meanwhile, place the remaining lemon juice and zest into a small pan with the sweetener and warm gently for 1 minute, add the honey and warm 1-2 more minutes until it becomes syrupy.

7. Drizzle the hot honey and lemon over the cooled cake and leave to soak for a few minutes before serving.

Recipe Tips

This cake is wonderful with limes or oranges instead of lemon (reduce the sweetener if using sweet oranges).

Great served with fresh berries and a blob of 0% fat Greek-style yogurt.

Freezing instructions: Slice, then wrap in foil to freeze (you can then use slices as required). May be a little crumbly when defrosted, but it will still taste delicious.

Nutrition:

KCal 118 Carbs 10.9g Fibre 0.4g Protein 3.1g Fat 6.8g Saturates 0.7g Sugars 1.9g Salt 0.4g

Spiced Apple And Raisin Muesli Bars

Servings: 16

Cooking Time: 20-25 Minutes

Ingredients:

- 2 bananas (100g each peeled weight)
- 2 apples, cored and finely chopped, but not peeled (125g each)
- 175g rolled oats
- 150ml apple juice
- 40g raisins
- 40g mixed seeds, such as sunflower and pumpkin
- 1 heaped tsp ground cinnamon
- 1 tsp rapeseed oil

Directions:

1. Preheat the oven to 180°C/ gas 4. With a fork, thoroughly mash the bananas, then beat them a little.
2. Add the apples, oats, apple juice, raisins, seeds and cinnamon. Mix well.
3. Oil a baking sheet and spread out the mixture to a depth of 2cm.
4. Bake in the oven for 15–20 minutes.
5. Allow to cool, cut into 16 portions and serve.

Recipe Tips

You can add sesame, hemp or poppy seeds, and linseeds to this recipe. Or, you could buy a bag of ready-mixed seeds.

Store at room temperature in an airtight container for a couple of days, or in the fridge for up to one week.

Nutrition:

KCal 91 Carbs 14.4g Fibre 1.6g Protein 2.2g Fat 2.3g Saturates 0.3g Sugars 6.5g Salt 0.01g Fruit/Veg Portion 0

Spiced Apple Polenta Bites

Servings: 25

Cooking Time: 16-20 Minutes

Ingredients:

- 300ml boiling water
- 20g sugar
- 8 stevia tablets
- 1 heaped tsp ground ginger
- 1 heaped tsp ground cinnamon
- half level tsp ground cloves
- 40g raisins
- 15g candied peel
- 100g instant polenta
- 1 unpeeled apple, cored and grated
- 1 egg, beaten
- 50ml rapeseed oil
- half tsp baking powder
- mini paper/foil baking cases
- 3 glacé cherries, 6 blanched almonds and 1 tsp pine nuts, to garnish

Directions:

1. Preheat the oven to 180°C/gas 4.
2. Add the water to a pan, along with the sugar, stevia,

ginger, cinnamon, cloves, raisins and candied peel. Stir and bring to boiling point, stirring until the sugar has dissolved.

3. Gradually stir in the polenta and keep stirring for 4–5 minutes until it has thickened, then remove from the heat.

4. In a bowl, mix the apple, egg, oil and baking powder together, then vigorously stir into the polenta.

5. Spoon into 25 cases and arrange on a baking sheet. Top each with either half a glacé cherry, an almond or a few pine nuts.

6. Place in the oven and bake for 16–20 minutes until lightly browned on top.

Nutrition:

KCal 50 Carbs 6.3g Fibre 0.4g Protein 0.9g Fat 2.3g Saturates 0.2g Sugars 2.9g Salt 0.04g

Spiced Citrus Teabread

Servings: 14

Cooking Time: 45 Minutes

Ingredients:

- 450g strong flour
- half tsp ground cinnamon
- 1 sachet easy-blend dried yeast
- 50g polyunsaturated spread
- 50g soft brown sugar
- grated zest and juice 1 lemon
- grated zest and juice 2 oranges
- 200g sultanas
- 100g ready-to-eat dried apricots, chopped
- 200g raisins
- 1 egg, beaten
- 1 tbsp milk

Directions:

1. Sift together the flour and cinnamon into a large bowl, then stir through the yeast. Rub in the spread, until the mixture resembles fine breadcrumbs.

2. Add the sugar, lemon and orange rind and the dried fruit. Mix together the lemon and orange juice with 100ml hot water, stir through the egg then work into the flour mixture. Form into a dough.

3. Tip the dough onto a lightly floured surface and knead for 5-6 minutes until smooth. Form into a neat round and put into a bowl. Cover with a tea towel and stand in a warm place for about 1 hour until doubled in size.

4. 'Knock back' the dough by kneading again for 1 minute then shape into a loaf, cover with lightly oiled clingfilm and allow to rise for another 30 minutes.

5. Preheat oven to 190°C/gas 5. Remove the film, mark 4 deep slashes into the bread and brush with the milk.

6. Bake for about 45 minutes, until golden and hollow when tapped. Leave to cool.

Recipe Tips

You could use mixed spice in place of the cinnamon.

Try with mixed vine fruits instead of raisins and sultanas.

Freezing instructions: Slice then wrap in foil to freeze. You can then defrost slices as required.

Nutrition:

KCal 252 Carbs 50.0g Fibre 2.5g Protein 5.8g Fat 2.6g

Saturates 0.6g Sugars 25.9g Salt 0.1g

Skewered Fruit With Dipping Sauces

Servings: 3

Cooking Time: 0 Minutes

Ingredients:

- For the kebabs:
- 400g mixed fruit, sliced
- For the sauce:
- 150g berries (any type)
- sugar-free sweetener, to taste
- 2 tbsp virtually fat-free fromage frais

Directions:

1. Simply thread the fruit onto cocktail sticks or skewers.

2. To make the sauce, place the strawberries and sweetener in a blender and blend until smooth, adding a little water if the sauce is too thick.

3. Spoon the berry sauce and the fromage frais into separate bowls and use as dips for the kebabs.

Recipe Tips

Use a soya-based yogurt instead of fromage frais if you are lactose-intolerant or vegan.

Nutrition:

KCal 102 Carbs 19.7g Fibre 4.0g Protein 2.3g Fat 0.6g

Saturates 0.1g Sugars 18.9g Salt 0.02g Fruit/Veg Portion 2

Rich Fruit Cake

Servings: 12

Cooking Time: 1.5 Hours

Ingredients:

- 75g sultanas
- 100g raisins
- 25g candied peel
- 100ml boiling water
- 1 medium banana, mashed
- 2 eggs, beaten
- 75ml rapeseed oil
- 1 medium courgette, grated (200g)
- 1 apple, grated
- 1 carrot, finely grated
- 150g wholemeal flour
- 1 tsp baking powder
- 3 tsp mixed spice
- 6 glacé cherries, halved
- 20g whole, blanched almonds

Directions:

1. Preheat the oven to 170°C/gas 3. Add the sultanas, raisins and peel to a bowl, cover with the boiling water and set aside.

2. Mix together the mashed banana, eggs and oil in a large bowl, and beat well.

3. Mix in the courgette, apple and carrot, then stir in the flour, baking powder and mixed spice. Next, add the dried fruit, plus soaking water.

4. Mix well and put into a 20cm cake tin lined with baking parchment, top with the cherries and

almonds. Cover with foil and bake in the oven for 1½ hours. Remove the foil 15–20 minutes before the end of the cooking time, then bake for the remainder of the time.

5. Test with a skewer or knife, which should come out clean when cooked, and remove from the oven.

Recipe Tips

You could easily make this cake with gluten-free flour, but you may need to add an extra 50ml liquid, depending on the type of flour you choose.

Any dried fruits work well – prunes, apricots, currants or mixed fruit.

Once cooked, you can drizzle with 1 tsp runny honey, if preferred.

Nutrition:

KCal 200 Carbs 25.2g Fibre 2.4g Protein 4.2g Fat 8.6g Saturates 0.8g Sugars 14.5g Salt 0.19g

Rhubarb Fool

Servings: 6

Cooking Time: 6 Minutes

Ingredients:

- 400g rhubarb, cut in 1cm chunks
- artificial sweetener to taste (equivalent to 8 tsp sugar, such as 8 stevia tablets, crushed)
- 150g 0% fat Greek yogurt
- 100g reduced-fat crème fraiche

Directions:

1. Add the rhubarb to a pan with 3 tbsp water. Bring to the boil, turn down the heat, add a lid and simmer for 6 minutes, stirring regularly, adding another tablespoon of water if it starts to stick. The rhubarb should be soft, but still hold its shape.

2. Transfer the rhubarb to a bowl and add the artificial sweetener. Mix well and taste adding a little more artificial sweetener if needed, then leave to cool. Remember the yogurt contains natural sugars so don't over sweeten.

3. In a bowl, mix the yogurt and crème fraiche together and fold in the rhubarb. Place in glasses and chill before serving.

Recipe Tips

Can be made in advance and kept in the fridge for a few hours. Or if you want to make it a day before serving, just chill the rhubarb separately and mix with the yogurt and crème fraiche when needed.

This recipe works well with other tart fruits, such as gooseberries or redcurrants.

You can use most fruit, although you won't need to sweeten it quite as much if the fruit is sweet. Try apricots, peaches, nectarines, raspberries or cherries.

For a vegan version, use unsweetened soy or coconut-based yoghurt.

Nutrition:

KCal 51 Carbs 2.8g Fibre 1.2g Protein 3.6g Fat 2.6g Saturates 1.7g Sugars 2.0g Salt 0.04g

Rhubarb And Ginger Sponge

Servings: 6

Cooking Time: 25-30 Minutes

Ingredients:

- 500g chopped rhubarb
- 2 tbsp water
- 2 tbsp granulated sweetener
- 2 eggs, beaten
- 2 tbsp low-fat yoghurt
- 3 tbsp rapeseed oil
- 100g wholemeal flour
- 1 heaped tsp ground ginger
- 1 tsp baking powder
- 100ml skimmed milk

Directions:

1. Preheat oven to 180°C / gas mark 4.

2. Add rhubarb to a microwave/oven-proof dish with the water. Cover with cling film, pierce, then microwave for 2-3 minutes until tender.

3. Mix in 1 tbsp of sweetener. Add more if needed according to taste.

4. Add the eggs to a bowl with the yogurt and oil, then beat well.

5. Stir in the flour, ginger, baking powder and remaining sweetener.

6. Beat in the milk to create a batter, then pour it over the rhubarb. Bake for 25-30 minutes until lightly golden on top.

Recipe Tips

Experiment with other fruits such as apples, pears, apricots or frozen berries.

Try adding other spices such as cinnamon or mixed spice - especially good with apple.

Freezing instructions: Suitable for freezing once cooked. Defrost in the fridge and reheat until piping hot.

Nutrition:

KCal 157 Carbs 13.8g Fibre 3.3g Protein 6.2g Fat 7.8g Saturates 1.0g Sugars 2.0g Salt 0.31g

Raspberry Shortbread Mess

Servings: 2

Ingredients:

- 150g raspberries
- 1tsp sugar free sweetener
- 2 shortbread fingers (39g total weight)
- 150g 0% Greek yogurt

Directions:

1. In a bowl, gently crush half the raspberries with a fork and mix with the sweetener.

2. In another bowl, crumble up the shortbread biscuits.

3. Reserve a couple of whole raspberries and a little crushed shortbread, to garnish.

4. Fold the remaining whole and crushed raspberries, plus the shortbread, into the yogurt.

5. Arrange in glasses or bowls, sprinkle with crushed shortbread and top with a raspberry.

Recipe Tips

This recipe works well with strawberries or blackberries, too. Or try chopped peaches or nectarines.

Try using a different biscuits, such as digestives or

ginger biscuits.

For a vegan version, use a soy or coconut-based dairy free alternative to the yogurt.

Freezing instructions: Remove from freezer a few minutes before serving.

Nutrition:

KCal 170 Carbs 17.5g Fibre 2.9g Protein 9.9g Fat 5.9g Saturates 3.5g Sugars 9.0g Salt 0.23g

Raspberry Fruit Spread

Servings: 10

Cooking Time: 2+ Hours

Ingredients:

- 200ml water
- 1 sachet sugar-free raspberry jelly crystals
- 3 tsp granulated sweetener
- 150g frozen raspberries

Directions:

1. Add the water and jelly to a jug, stir in the sweetener, then add half the raspberries. Gently mash them with a fork to break them up.

2. Stir in the remaining raspberries, then place in the fridge in a jar or airtight container until set.

3. Store in the fridge - keeps for 5 days.

Recipe Tips

This method works well with other fruits such as strawberries or blackberries.

Using frozen fruit will make the jelly cool and set quicker than it would with fresh fruit.

For a vegetarian or vegan version use an unflavoured

seaweed based gelling agent and use sugar-free squash and sweetener to create a fruit liquid.

Chop the jam up with a spoon before eating to make it easier to spread.

Nutrition:

KCal 12 Carbs 1.0g Fibre 0.5g Protein 1.5g Fat 0.0g Saturates 0.0g Sugars 0.7g Salt 0.0g

Raspberry Frozen Yogurt

Servings: 11   Prep 10 minutes + 1.5 to 2 hours to freeze

Ingredients:

- 300g fresh raspberries
- 500g Greek yogurt
- 50g caster sugar

Directions:

1. Place half of the raspberries into a blender or food processor and purée.

2. Mix together the yogurt and sugar and transfer to a freezer-proof container, freeze for 1 hour, stir well then gently fold through the remaining raspberries and the raspberry purée.

3. Return to the freezer for 30 minutes, then mix again with a fork and and return to the freezer. Freeze a further 30 minutes until solid.

4. Remove from freezer for 5 minutes before serving

Recipe Tips

You could use most fruits with this method, try mango, blueberry, strawberry or nectarine.

If using an ice-cream scoop to serve, dip it into hot water between scoops for easy serving.

Nutrition:

KCal 57 Carbs 4.0g Fibre 1.2g Protein 6.7g Fat 1.4g Saturates 0.8g Sugars 3.9g Salt 0.05g

Quick Fruit Bread

Servings: 10

Cooking Time: 25 Minutes

Ingredients:

- 1 tsp sunflower oil
- 75g raisins
- 1 heaped tsp ground cinnamon
- 1 banana (approx. 100g peeled)
- 4 tbsp low-fat natural yogurt
- 175g wholemeal flour
- 1 tsp bicarbonate of soda

Directions:

1. Preheat the oven to 180°C/gas 4. Use the sunflower oil to lightly grease a 1lb loaf tin (approx 19cm x 10cm).

2. Place the raisins in a bowl with the cinnamon and 100ml boiling water. Set aside.

3. In another bowl, mash the banana and mix with the yogurt.

4. In a large bowl, mix the flour and bicarbonate of soda together.

5. Add the banana and yogurt mix to the flour mixture. Add the raisins and water, and mix thoroughly. Pour the mixture into the loaf tin.

6. Bake for 25 minutes until firm and golden. The bread is cooked when a knife inserted into the centre comes out clean.

Recipe Tips

Once the wet ingredients are added to the dry ones, you activate the bicarbonate of soda, so pop it into the oven quickly for maximum lightness.

You could use any dried fruit instead of raisins, such as chopped apricots, sultanas, prunes or mixed fruit.

Try adding a teaspoon of mixed spice or a pinch of ground cloves.

Freeze, wrapped in foil or greaseproof paper, for up to three months.

You can freeze this bread, whole or cut into slices, for up to three months. Simply wrap in foil, put into freezer bags and label. This fruity bread can be toasted from frozen.

Nutrition:

KCal 98 Carbs 19.0g Fibre 2.4g Protein 2.7g Fat 0.8g Saturates 0.1g Sugars 7.3g Salt 0.3g

Power Porridge

Servings: 2

Cooking Time: 5 Minutes

Ingredients:

- 30g rolled oats
- 30g buckwheat flakes
- 30g quinoa flakes
- 400ml water
- 1–2 tsp granulated sweetener, if desired
- 160g frozen mixed berries, defrosted
- 10g sunflower seeds, toasted
- 10g flaked almonds
- 10g pumpkin seeds
- 50ml skimmed milk, to serve (optional)

Directions:

1. Place the oats, buckwheat and quinoa flakes in a small pan, cover with the water, add the sweetener (if using), and then place over a low heat. Cook for 3–4 minutes.

2. Divide the porridge between 2 bowls, and top with the berries and toasted seeds. Serve with milk, if desired.

Nutrition:

KCal 290 Carbs 38.1g Fibre 5.4g Protein 10.5g Fat 9.7g Saturates 1.2g Sugars 7.0g Salt 0.06g Fruit/Veg Portion 1

Popcorn

Servings: 10

Cooking Time: 3 Minutes

Ingredients:

- 75g popping corn
- juice and zest 1 orange
- 1 level tsp powdered ginger
- 3 tsp granulated sweetener

Directions:

1. Heat a large deep pan with a lid, add half (or a third, depending on the size of your pan) of the popping corn and cover. Shake regularly and after 2-3 minutes you'll hear the corn start to pop – don't be tempted to open the lid! Keep shaking until the popping stops.

2. Put the popped corn into a large bowl and discard any corn that hasn't popped. Repeat until all your corn is done.

3. Meanwhile, in another saucepan warm the orange juice, ginger and sweetener and until dissolved. Mix until it reaches boiling point then heat for 2-3 minutes until it becomes sticky and the volume is reduced by three quarters.

4. Stir in the zest and add the popcorn, mixing well so it is all coated.

5. Spread onto a tray and leave to dry completely before bagging it up.

Recipe Tips

Don't put too much corn in at once – cook in batches as it expands a lot. Don't open the lid while it's popping as it will pop out all over the kitchen.

Take care not to let the pan dry completely as you need enough sauce to coat the popcorn, but if the sauce is too wet your popcorn will be soggy.

Make sure the popcorn is thoroughly cooled before you bag it.

Try adding a good pinch of spice, such as cinnamon or nutmeg.

If you put this sticky orange and ginger popcorn into bags and tie with a ribbon, it's a healthy treat for Halloween.

Nutrition:

KCal 34 Carbs 6.4g Fibre 0.3g Protein 1.0g Fat 0.4g Saturates 0.0g Sugars 0.6g Salt 0.0g Fruit/Veg Portion 0

Pink Poached Pears

Servings: 4

Cooking Time: 45 Minutes

Ingredients:

- 4 firm, slightly under ripe pears, peeled with stalk left intact
- 150ml sugar-free blackcurrant cordial
- 500-600ml boiling water (enough to cover the pears)
- 2 star anise
- 1 cinnamon stick

Directions:

1. Peel pears and core from the base using a small knife or vegetable peeler. Trim the base flat so the pears stand up.

2. Add the pears to a pan with cordial diluted 3:1, making sure they are fully immersed.

3. Add star anise and the cinnamon stick, then bring to the boil. Turn down the heat and simmer for 20-30 minutes until the pears are tender.

4. Remove from pan and set aside. Boil the liquid for 10-15 minutes until the liquid is reduced to about 200ml, then remove the star anise and cinnamon stick.

5. Place the pears on a serving dish and drizzle with the sauce. Serve with a dollop of low-fat yogurt or non-dairy alternative.

Recipe Tips

Works very well with apples in place of pears.

Try using a different cordial or add a few slices of fresh ginger or 2 cloves.

Nutrition:

KCal 75 Carbs 16.0g Fibre 4.0g Protein 0.5g Fat 0.1g Saturates 0.0g Sugars 16.0g Salt 0.0g Fruit/Veg Portion 1

Pear And Almond Traybake

Servings: 12

Cooking Time: 20-22 Minutes

Ingredients:

- 3 pears, peeled and quartered
- 2 medium eggs
- 75g caster sugar (reserve 1 tsp to top)
- 100ml rapeseed oil (use 1 tsp for greasing)
- 1 tsp almond essence
- 100g wholemeal flour
- 1 tsp baking powder
- 20g flaked almonds

Directions:

1. Preheat the oven to 180°C/gas 4 and lightly grease a baking tray (approx 20cm x 25cm) with 1 tsp of the rapeseed oil.

2. In a bowl, beat the eggs, sugar, rapeseed oil and almond essence together.

3. Add the flour and baking powder, mix well and add to the baking tray.

4. Arrange the pears on top, sprinkle with the almonds and the reserved tsp of sugar. Bake for 20-22 minutes. The cake is cooked when a knife inserted into the centre comes out clean.

Recipe Tips

Tinned pears also work well in this recipe.

You could use other fruit such as apples, peaches, nectarines, cherries or plums in this traybake.

Try using a different essences, such as vanilla or lemon or add some grated lemon or orange zest.

Freeze wrapped in foil or greaseproof in labelled freezer bags for up to three months.

Nutrition:

KCal 147 Carbs 14.8g Fibre 1.6g Protein 2.8g Fat 8.1g Saturates 0.8g Sugars 9.2g Salt 0.14g

Summer Berry Pavlova

Servings: 5

Cooking Time: 1 Hours 45 Minutes

Ingredients:

- 1/2 box fresh strawberries (160g)
- Small punnet fresh raspberries (120g)
- Small punnet fresh blueberries (120g)
- 4 tbsp water
- 3.5 tbsp granulated sweetener
- 1 tsp lemon juice
- 6 egg whites
- 1 tsp cream of tartar
- 4 tsp cornflour
- 200g 0% fat Greek yogurt
- sweetener, to taste
- few sprigs mint, to serve

Directions:

1. Put the water, granulated sweetener and lemon juice in a small pan over a low heat until the liquid has reduced and begins to look sticky.

2. Meanwhile, put the egg whites and cream of tartar in a bowl, and slowly whisk together until they form soft peaks.

3. Slowly pour the sweetener mixture into the beaten

egg whites.

4. Gently add the cornflour and continue to mix until the egg whites are stiff.

5. On a parchment-lined baking tray, spread or pipe the meringue to form a bowl, about 20-25cm (10 ins) across.

6. Bake in a cool oven, 100°C/gas ¼ for about 1 hour 20 minutes, until it is firm and just beginning to colour. Open the oven door and leave the meringue in the oven until it is cool.

7. When cool, carefully place the meringue on your serving plate.

8. Combine a third of the fruit with the yogurt, adding sweetener if needed. Pile into the meringue and top with the remaining berries and a few sprigs of mint.

Recipe Tips

If your meringue starts to brown before it is cooked, open the oven door for a few minutes to reduce the heat. Don't fill your meringue until just before serving – it will go soggy if it's left too long with the berry filling. However, you can make the yogurt/fruit mixture in advance and refrigerate until needed.

Nutrition:

KCal 86 Carbs 10.7g Fibre 2.4g Protein 9.0g Fat 0.3g Saturates 0.0g Sugars 6.5g Salt 0.22g Fruit/Veg Portion 1

Orange Fruit Spread

Servings: 12

Cooking Time: 2 hours

Ingredients:

- 3 medium oranges
- 200ml boiling water
- 23g sachet sugar-free orange jelly crystals

Directions:

1. Finely zest the oranges, then add the zest to a jug with boiling water.

2. Stir in the jelly sachet until fully dissolved.

3. Cut the pith from the orange, then segment the flesh leaving the pith behind. Roughly chop and add to the jug.

4. Squeeze the core of the orange to get any juice out, then add that to the jug.

5. Allow to cool, then put into a large jar, mix, then seal and refrigerate for at least 2-3 hours. Store in the fridge - keeps for 5 days.

Recipe Tips

Chop the marmalade up with a spoon before eating to make spreading easier.

For a vegetarian or vegan version, use an unflavoured, seaweed-based gelling agent and use sugar-free squash and sweetener.

Nutrition:

KCal 16 Carbs 2.3g Fibre 0.5g Protein 1.4g Fat 0.1g Saturates 0.0g Sugars 2.1g Salt 0.0g Fruit/Veg Portion 0

One Crust Fruit Pie

Servings: 4

Cooking Time: 30 Minutes

Ingredients:

- 150g ready-made shortcrust pastry
- a little flour, for rolling
- 2 tbsp semi-skimmed milk
- 1 tbsp semolina
- 2 cooking apples, peeled, cored and chopped
- 100g blackberries
- 1 tbsp demerara sugar

Directions:

1. Preheat the oven to 200°C/gas 6.
2. Flour the worktop and roll out the pastry to a round 25cm in diameter. Brush with a little of the milk and sprinkle over the semolina.
3. Mix together the apples, blackberries and half the sugar and place onto the pastry, leaving a 6cm gap around the edge.
4. Fold up the edges of the pastry and press together (the top of the pie should remain open) brush with the remaining milk and sprinkle over the remaining sugar.
5. Bake for 25–30 minutes until golden and the fruit is tender. Serve with a little crème fraiche, yogurt or ice-cream.

Recipe Tips

If you like a juicer and softer pie, cook the apple and blackberries for 3–4 mins in a pan with 1 tbsp water and spread over the pastry.

You could also use pears, apricots, peaches, nectarines or cherries.

Nutrition:

KCal 256 Carbs 30.6g Fibre 4.1g Protein 3.6g Fat 12.3g Saturates 4.5g Sugars 14.1g Salt 0.22g

Mulled Apple Juice

Servings: 12

Cooking Time: 15 Minutes

Ingredients:

- 2 oranges, sliced
- 2 or 3 cinnamon sticks
- 3cm fresh ginger root, peeled and thinly sliced
- 2 star anise, and extra to serve
- 6 whole cloves, and extra to serve
- 1L 100% pure apple juice

Directions:

1. Place 1 of the oranges with 1 of the cinnamon sticks, ginger, star anise and cloves in a saucepan with a litre of boiling water, and simmer gently for ten minutes.
2. Add the apple juice and gently heat for 3-4 minutes, taking care not to boil.
3. Strain, pour into a jug or individual glasses and garnish with cinnamon sticks, slices of orange, cloves and star anise.

Recipe Tips

You could make this recipe with no added sugar cranberry juice for a ruby-red seasonal drink.

Nutrition:

KCal 41 Carbs 9.7g Fibre 0.3g Protein 0.3g Fat 0.0g   0

Saturates 0.0g Sugars 9.7g Salt 0.01g Fruit/Veg Portion

LAMB RECIPES

Lamb And Sweet Potato Hotpot

Servings: 6

Cooking Time: 2 Hours

Ingredients:

- 1 tsp rapeseed oil
- 500g lean lamb leg steaks, cut into chunks
- 3 medium onions, chopped
- 2 leeks, chopped
- 3 medium carrots, chopped
- 300g sweet potatoes, peeled and chopped into large cubes, plus 150g sweet potatoes cut into thin slices (total weight 400g)
- 1 tbsp plain flour
- 1 low-salt lamb stock cube dissolved in 500ml boiling water
- 50g split peas
- bay leaf
- good pinch white pepper

Directions:

1. Add the oil to a saucepan over a low to medium heat, add the lamb and heat for 5 minutes.
2. Add the onion and gently brown for 5-7 minutes, stirring regularly.
3. Add the leeks, carrots and cubed sweet potatoes, stir 2-3 minutes.
4. Sprinkle the vegetables with flour and mix well ensuring all pieces are coated.
5. Stir in the stock and add the split peas, bay leaf and white pepper.
6. Cover and simmer gently for 45 minutes, stirring occasionally, and adding water if more liquid is needed. After about 30 minutes preheat your oven to 180C/gas 4.
7. Remove from the heat and add to an ovenproof dish. Arrange the sweet potato slices on top. Bake for 15-20 minutes until the potato is golden brown and crisping at the edges.

Recipe Tips

You could make this dish with chicken pieces, pork or beef.

Any root vegetables work well – try a combination of carrots, swede and turnip.

Freezing instructions: Freeze in portions then defrost in the fridge, or defrost in a microwave, taking care to stir regularly.

Nutrition:

KCal 288   Carbs 28.4g   Fibre 6.8g   Protein 21.3g

Fat 8.4g   Saturates 3.1g   Sugars 10.3g   Salt 0.3g

Fruit/Veg Portion 2

Lamb Biryani

Servings: 6

Cooking Time: 1 Hour 15 Minutes

Ingredients:

- 1 tbsp oil
- 4 onions, sliced
- 750g boneless leg of lamb, cubed
- 4 cloves garlic, crushed
- 1.5 tsp fresh ginger, peeled and grated
- 1 stick cinnamon
- 3 cardamom pods
- 8 cloves
- 8 black peppercorns
- 1 tbsp chilli powder
- 1 tbsp ground coriander
- 1 x 150g tub low-fat natural yogurt
- half tsp saffron, soaked in 3 tbsp boiling water
- 450g basmati rice, cooked according to pack instructions

Directions:

1. Heat the oil in a large pan, add the onion and fry for 3-4 minutes until lightly golden. Remove ¼ of the onion and set aside.

2. Add the lamb, garlic, ginger, cinnamon stick, cardamom, cloves and peppercorns to the pan and fry for 8-10 minutes until the lamb is lightly browned all over.

3. Stir the chilli powder and ground coriander into 2 bsps boiling water, then pour into the pan. Cover the pan and cook the meat over a low heat. Cook for 40-45 minutes until the meat is tender.

4. Preheat the oven to 150°C/gas 2. Add the yogurt to the pan and stir. Meanwhile, place the reserved onion in a pan and continue to fry for 5-6 minutes until dark brown.

5. Place ⅓ of the rice into the base of a heavy casserole dish, drizzle over a little of the saffron mixture. Layer over half of the meat mixture and cover with another ⅓ of the rice and sprinkle with a little saffron mixture. Repeat, finishing with a layer of rice and drizzling with saffron. Press down lightly. Place the onion on top.

6. Cover the pan with a tight fitting lid and cook for 10 minutes. Remove from the oven, sprinkle with fresh coriander and serve.

Recipe Tips

You could use chicken or pork for this dish.

For a vegetarian version, add a selection of chopped vegetables such as peppers, aubergines and mushrooms in place of lamb. They will only need 5 minutes to cook before adding to the rice.

Freezing instructions: Suitable for freezing once cooked. Chill quickly. Defrost in the fridge and reheat thoroughly until piping hot throughout. Eat immediately and discard any leftovers.

Nutrition:

KCal 538   Carbs 69.3g   Fibre 3.9g   Protein 34.1g

Fat 12.9g   Saturates 4.9g   Sugars 7.9g   Salt 0.5g

Fruit/Veg Portion 1

Italian-Style Braised Lamb Steaks

Servings: 4

Cooking Time: 60 Minutes

Ingredients:

- 2 tsp rapseseed oil
- 4 red onions, quartered
- 4 lamb steaks (approx. 500g) fat trimmed
- 1 tbsp flour
- 4 cloves garlic, sliced
- large sprig rosemary, torn into pieces, plus a little to serve or 1 level tsp dried rosemary
- 1 heaped tsp oregano
- 1 lamb stock cube dissolved in 500ml water
- 1 x 400g can chopped tomatoes
- 1 tbsp balsamic vinegar
- good pinch pepper

Directions:

1. Preheat the oven to 180°C/gas 4. Add 1 tsp of the oil to a pan over a low-medium heat, add the onions and gently brown for 3-4 minutes, turning regularly. Set aside.

2. Coat the lamb in flour and add the remaining oil to the pan. Cook for 2-3 mins on each side.

3. Return the onions to the pan, add the garlic, rosemary and oregano. Stir in the stock and bring to a gentle boil.

4. Add the tomatoes, balsamic vinegar and pepper.

5. Place in an ovenproof dish and cook for 45-50 minutes. Garnish with a little fresh rosemary and serve.

Recipe Tips

You could cook the whole dish on the hob if you prefer – just simmer gently for 45-50 minutes. Take care not to boil dry so add a little water if required.

Works well with skinless chicken thighs.

Freezing instructions: Suitable for freezing once cooked. Defrost in the fridge or microwave and reheat until piping hot throughout.

Nutrition:

KCal 312   Carbs 20.0g   Fibre 4.8g   Protein 28.8g

Fat 11.9g   Saturates 4.6g   Sugars 13.7g   Salt 0.63g

Fruit/Veg Portion 3

Irish Stew And Colcannon

Servings: 4

Cooking Time: 1.5–2 Hours

Ingredients:

- For the stew:
- 1 tsp olive oil
- 1 large onion, peeled and cut into large chunks
- 450g lean lamb, cubed
- 650g potatoes, peeled and cut into large chunks
- 2 carrots, peeled and cut into large chunks
- 1 stock cube
- dash Worcestershire sauce
- 1 tbsp gravy powder
- good pinch mixed dried herbs
- For the colcannon:
- 650g sweet potatoes, peeled and chopped
- 2 tbsp semi-skimmed milk
- 1 tbsp reduced-fat polyunsaturated margarine
- freshly ground black pepper
- half savoy cabbage, finely sliced
- 1 bunch spring onions, roughly chopped

Directions:

1. Heat the oil in a large, flame-proof casserole dish, add the onions and lamb and fry for 3–4 minutes, until the meat is browned.

2. Add the remaining stew ingredients and enough water to cover the contents. Bring to the boil, cover and simmer very gently for 1½–2 hours, until the meat is tender.

3. Meanwhile, make the colcannon. Place the potatoes into a large pan of boiling water and cook for 10–12 minutes until tender. Drain, mash together with the milk and margarine, and season with plenty of black pepper.

4. Cook the cabbage in a pan of boiling water until tender, drain and stir a quarter of it through the mash with the spring onions.

5. Serve the remaining cabbage with the stew and colcannon.

Recipe Tips

You could use beef, pork or venison instead of lamb.

If using fatty meat, cook the dish the day before, refrigerate and when cooled then skim the fat from the top of the dish before reheating.

Freezing instructions: Suitable for freezing once cooked. Defrost in the fridge or microwave and reheat until piping hot throughout.

Nutrition:

KCal 577   Carbs 75.1g   Fibre 14.0g   Protein 30.6g

Fat 14.1g   Saturates 5.2g   Sugars 20.8g   Salt 1.75g

Fruit/Veg Portion 3

Harira

Servings: 6

Cooking Time: 1 Hour and 30 Minutes

Ingredients:

- 1 tbsp olive oil
- 200g onion, chopped
- 500g lean lamb, cut into 1cm cubes
- 3 peppers – red, yellow and green, chopped
- 2 carrots, diced
- 1 aubergine, chopped into 2cm cubes
- 3 cloves garlic, chopped
- 1 heaped tsp paprika
- 1 heaped tsp cumin
- 1 rounded tsp turmeric
- 1 heaped tsp cinnamon
- 1 x 400g can chopped tomatoes
- 1 vegetable stock cube (gluten-free)
- 1.5 litre boiling water
- 1 x 400g can chickpeas, drained
- 1 x 400g can green lentils, drained
- 170g pot 0% fat Greek yogurt
- 30g bunch fresh coriander, chopped
- lemon wedges

Directions:

1. Heat the oil in a large pan, add the onion and cook for 5 minutes until starting to brown.

2. Add the lamb and cook for a further 7 minutes, stirring regularly.

3. Now add the peppers, carrots and aubergine, mix well and cook for 5 minutes.

4. Next, add the garlic, paprika, cumin, turmeric and cinnamon. Mix well, then add the tomatoes, crumble in the stock cube and stir in the water.

5. Bring to the boil, stir and cover. Turn down the heat and simmer gently for 1 hour, then add the chickpeas and lentils, including their water. Mix well and cook for a further 30 minutes.

6. Meanwhile, mix the yogurt and coriander together.

7. Ladle the soup into bowls and top with a dollop of the coriander yogurt and a squeeze of lemon.

Recipe Tips

For a veggie version, swap the lamb for a pack of marinated or smoked tofu and a can of mixed beans. Harira also works well with chicken or beef.

Keeps in the fridge for 2-3 days – it tastes even better the day after you've made it.

Freezing instructions: Suitable for freezing once cooked. Defrost in the fridge or microwave and reheat until piping hot throughout.

Nutrition:

KCal 308   Carbs 23.9g   Fibre 8.0g   Protein 25.7g

Fat 10.4g   Saturates 3.3g   Sugars 11.7g   Salt 0.73g

Fruit/Veg Portion 4

Lamb Curry

Servings: 6

Cooking Time: 2.5 hours

Ingredients:

- 2 tsp sunflower oil
- 400g diced lean lamb
- 3 onions, chopped
- 4 carrots, chopped
- 2 x 400g tins chopped tomatoes
- 1 tbsp tomato puree
- 2-3 tsp curry powder
- 1-3 Scotch bonnet chillies, finely chopped (according to how hot you like it)
- 6cm fresh ginger, grated
- 1 level tsp allspice
- 1 tbsp chopped parsley
- 1 low-salt vegetable or chicken stock cube
- 1 litre water
- 1 tbsp chopped coriander

Directions:

1. Heat the oil in a pan and add the lamb and onions. Cook for 5 minutes stirring regularly until starting to brown.

2. Add all the other ingredients, except the coriander, stir and bring to the boil. Put the lid on, reduce the heat and simmer gently for 2–2.5 hours stirring regularly, until the lamb is tender. Add a little more water if needed.

3. Serve with a sprinkle of coriander.

Recipe Tips

For a lower fat version, use chicken thighs – they will cook more quickly so reduce the cooking time by an hour.

Be warned, Scotch bonnet chillies may be very small – but they're also very hot!

Freezing instructions: Suitable for freezing once cooked. Defrost in the fridge or microwave and reheat until piping hot throughout.

Nutrition:

KCal 206   Carbs 16.5g   Fibre 4.9g   Protein 15.7g

Fat 7.5g   Saturates 2.6g   Sugars 14.0g   Salt 0.28g

Fruit/Veg Portion 3

Fillet Of Lamb With Minted Couscous

Servings: 4

Cooking Time: 20 Minutes

Ingredients:

- 450g lean lamb fillet
- freshly ground black pepper
- 2 tbsp redcurrant jelly
- 400ml vegetable stock (use gluten-free vegetable stock to make this recipe gluten-free)
- 2 tsp ground coriander
- 2 tsp ground cumin
- 175g couscous (use quinoa to make this recipe

gluten-free)

- 1 tbsp chopped fresh mint
- 4 tomatoes, chopped
- 2 tbsp parsley, chopped
- juice and zest 1 lemon

Directions:

1. Place the lamb on a baking tray and season with black pepper.

2. Heat the redcurrant jelly and pour over the lamb. Use a pastry bush to spread the jelly all over.

3. Cook the lamb under a hot grill for 10-15 minutes. Remove from the grill, cover with foil and allow to rest for 5 minutes.

4. Meanwhile, bring the vegetable stock to the boil and add the spices. Add the couscous, remove from the heat and cover with a lid. Leave to steam for 1 minute then fluff up the grains with a fork.

5. Stir in the chopped mint tomatoes, parsley, lemon juice and zest and pile onto serving plates.

6. Carve the lamb into thin slices and arrange on top of the couscous.

Recipe Tips

You could also use chicken breast or pork fillet with this recipe.

Freezing instructions: Freeze couscous and lamb separately. Defrost in the fridge or microwave and reheat until piping hot throughout.

Nutrition:

KCal 383   Carbs 40.4g   Fibre 4.0g   Protein 29.6g

Fat 10.6g   Saturates 4.1g   Sugars 8.2g   Salt 0.22g

Fruit/Veg Portion 1

Doner Kebabs

Servings: 4

Cooking Time: 30 Minutes

Ingredients:

- 1 heaped tsp oregano
- 1 tsp ground cinnamon
- half tsp ground cumin
- half tsp chilli flakes
- good pinch white pepper
- 2 cloves garlic, crushed
- grated zest and juice half lemon
- 1 egg, lightly beaten
- half slice wholemeal bread, crumbled
- 250g 10% fat minced lamb
- 4 wholemeal pitta breads (70g each)
- 4 large servings salad (cucumber, 100g iceberg lettuce, 300g tomatoes and 150g red onion)
- juice half lemon, to serve

Directions:

1. Add the oregano, cinnamon, cumin, chilli, pepper, garlic, lemon zest and juice to a bowl, along with the egg and crumbled bread. Mix well with a fork, breaking up the bread further.

2. Mix in the lamb and set aside for 10 minutes. Mix

again and shape into a loaf about 6cm in diameter and 13.5cm in length.

3. Place on a baking sheet and cook in a preheated oven 190°C/gas 5 for 25–30 minutes.

4. Allow to cool for 5 minutes, then slice thinly, and stuff into pitta breads full of salad. Drizzle with lemon juice and serve.

Recipe Tips

You can use any salad you like. To add a great crunch, use shredded raw cabbage, lettuce, red onion and cucumber, tossed in lemon juice.

For the sauces (pictured): Tahini sauce: Add 2 tsp tahini to a dish and gradually mix in 3 tbsp low-fat yogurt and pinch white pepper. Tomato relish: Mix a finely chopped large tomato with 1 tbsp ketchup and dash of chilli sauce.

Nutrition:

KCal 360   Carbs 38.5g   Fibre 8.5g   Protein 25.1g

Fat 9.7g   Saturates 3.2g   Sugars 7.2g   Salt 1.09g

Fruit/Veg Portion 1

PORK RECIPES

Spicy Ginger And Garlic Pork With Pak Choi

Servings: 2

Cooking Time: 12 Minutes

Ingredients:

- 180g pork fillet, trim fat and cut into 1cm-thick slices
- 4 cloves garlic, crushed
- 6cm fresh ginger, chopped
- 1–2 small red chillies, finely sliced
- juice half lime
- 2 tsp Chinese five-spice
- 2 tsp toasted sesame oil
- 3–4 heads pak choi
- 1 tsp rapeseed oil
- 1 bunch spring onions, chopped into 3cm-long pieces

Directions:

1. Add the pork to a bowl with the garlic, ginger, chilli, lime juice, Chinese five-spice and 1 tsp of the sesame oil. Mix well and set aside for at least 5 minutes to marinate (you could leave for 2 hours or overnight in the fridge).

2. Roughly chop the pak choi stems, leaving the leafy top intact, and set aside.

3. Add the rapeseed oil to a wok or pan then add the pork, any remaining marinade, and cook for 1–2 minutes each side.

4. Add the spring onions and chopped pak choi stems (retaining the leaves). Stir for 2–3 minutes.

5. Now add the leafy pak choi tops and the remaining 1 tsp of sesame oil. Stir fry for a further minute, then serve.

Recipe Tips

Chicken, turkey, beef or prawns would also work well with this recipe.

If the food starts to stick or the pan gets too hot when stir-frying if stick, add 1 tbsp water and continue to cook.

Nutrition:

KCal 211   Carbs 8.6g   Fibre 4.6g   Protein 23.1g   Fat 8.3g   Saturates 2.0g   Sugars 6.8g   Salt 0.31g   Fruit/Veg Portion 2

Pork With Creamy Leek Sauce

Servings: 4

Cooking Time: 10-12 Minutes

Ingredients:

- 2 tsp rapeseed oil
- 4 pork escalopes (400g)
- 2–3 leeks, chopped (400g)
- 3 heaped tsp Dijon mustard
- 2 heaped tsp plain flour
- 500ml skimmed milk
- pinch pepper

Directions:

1. Add the oil to a non-stick frying pan over a medium heat. Add the pork and cook for 2-3 minutes each side (to brown the outside). Remove from the pan and reserve.

2. Add the leeks to the pan and stir for 3-4 minutes, add the mustard and mix well. Next, sprinkle the flour over the leeks and mix well.

3. Slowly add the milk, stirring constantly until the sauce starts to thicken. Cook for another minute.

4. Put the pork escalopes back into the pan with the sauce, bring to a gentle simmer and cook for another 3-4 minutes, adding a dash more milk or water if the sauce becomes too thick.

5. Make sure the pork is cooked right through, season and serve.

Recipe Tips

You can also make this dish with turkey escalopes or chicken breasts.

For a rich and delicious vegetarian version of this recipe, try replacing the pork with a selection of mushrooms (400g).

Suitable for freezing once cooked. Then defrost thoroughly to serve or reheat until piping hot throughout. The sauce may separate but is still taste the same and is perfectly fine to eat.

Nutrition:

KCal 223   Carbs 10.7g   Fibre 3.0g   Protein 28.3g
Fat 6.7g   Saturates 1.8g   Sugars 8.1g   Salt 0.58g
Fruit/Veg Portion 1

Pork Chops With Roasted Pear, Apple And New Potatoes

Servings: 2

Cooking Time: 45-50 Minutes

Ingredients:

- 1 tsp rapeseed oil
- 2 lean pork chops (approx. 125g each), fat trimmed off
- freshly ground black pepper
- 1 eating apple, quartered and cored
- 1 large pear, quartered and cored
- 200g new potatoes, cut into chunks
- 1 small onion, cut into wedges
- grated rind and juice 1 orange
- 1 tsp fresh thyme or half tsp dried
- 1 tbsp wholegrain mustard
- 2 tbsp half-fat crème fraiche

Directions:

1. Preheat the oven to 180°C/ gas mark 4. Heat the oil in a frying pan, trim any fat from the pork chops, sprinkle with pepper and add to the pan, fry for 1–2 minutes on each side until golden.

2. Place in an ovenproof dish and add the apple, pear, potatoes and onion.

3. Mix together the orange rind and juice, thyme and mustard and pour over.

4. Cover the dish with foil and bake for 20 minutes, then remove the foil and mix well before baking for a further 20-30 minutes.

5. Stir through the crème fraîche and serve with vegetables such as wilted spinach.

Recipe Tips

You could use dried sage rather than thyme, or add a kick with English mustard instead of wholegrain.

For a veggie version, replace the pork with chunks of beetroot, carrot and butternut squash. Sprinkle with feta 10 minutes before the end of the cooking time.

Nutrition:

KCal 386   Carbs 39.0g   Fibre 6.4g   Protein 31.5g
Fat 10.1g   Saturates 3.6g   Sugars 23.9g   Salt 0.53g
Fruit/Veg Portion 3

Pork, Barley And Carrot Casserole

Servings: 4

Cooking Time: 1 Hour 15 Minutes

Ingredients:

- 1 tbsp sunflower oil
- 2 onions, diced
- 350g pork, cubed
- 300g Chantenay carrots, washed and left whole (no need to peel)
- 150g mushrooms, quartered
- 2 garlic cloves, crushed
- 1 tsp dried thyme
- 2 tsp wholemeal flour
- good pinch pepper
- 40g pearl barley
- 1 heaped tsp Dijon mustard
- 1 low-salt vegetable or chicken stock cube, dissolved in 1 litre water

Directions:

1. Preheat the oven to 180°C/gas 4. Add the oil and onions to a pan and cook until softened, but not browned.

2. Add the pork and cook for a further 2-3 minutes, stirring until the meat starts to brown.

3. Add the carrots, mushrooms, garlic, thyme, flour and seasoning, stir for 2-3 minutes, then add the barley, mustard and stock. Mix well, bring to the boil and transfer to an overproof casserole dish.

4. Put the lid on the casserole dish and place in the middle of the oven for 60-70 minutes. (Alternatively,

you can carry on cooking on the hob, if you add a lid and turn the heat down low.)

Recipe Tips

If using fatty meat, cook the casserole and then refrigerate overnight. You can then remove the fat easily from the top of the dish and reheat the casserole before serving.

Pearl barley is high in soluble fibre – the fibre that helps control blood glucose and cholesterol levels.

With a low glycaemic index, pearl barley is also a good alternative to other starchy carbohydrate foods.

Freezing instructions: Suitable for freezing once cooked. Defrost thoroughly to serve or reheat until piping hot throughout.

Nutrition:

KCal 271   Carbs 25.0g   Fibre 4.6g   Protein 23.0g
Fat 7.7g   Saturates 1.7g   Sugars 9.1g   Salt 0.97g
Fruit/Veg Portion 2

Pork Chilindron

Servings: 4

Cooking Time: 45 Minutes

Ingredients:

- 2 tsp rapeseed oil
- 1 pork tenderloin (approx. 400g), cut into 4 pieces
- 3 red onions, chopped
- 2 red peppers, chopped
- 4 cloves garlic, crushed
- 2–3 tsp smoked paprika (dulce/sweet)
- 1 tsp dried rosemary
- 400g tin tomatoes
- 1 low-salt vegetable stock cube (in 400ml boiling water)
- 320g broccoli florets

Directions:

1. Heat the oil in a pan and add the pork pieces. Brown the pork all over, remove from the pan and set aside.

2. Add the onions and peppers to the pan and stir for 3–4 minutes. Next, add the garlic, paprika, rosemary and tomatoes. Stir in the stock and bring to the boil. Cover and simmer for 15 minutes.

3. Return the pork to the pan and bring back to the boil. Turn down the heat and simmer for 20 minutes until the pork is tender.

4. Meanwhile, steam the broccoli and set aside.

5. Remove the pork and leave to stand for 5 minutes. Slice the meat thinly, and arrange on plates with the sauce and the broccoli.

Recipe Tips

You could use chicken or lamb neck fillets with this dish rather than pork. This dish also works well served with beans, chickpeas or lentils.

Nutrition:

KCal 269   Carbs 18.9g   Fibre 8.7g   Protein 28.5g

Fat 6.9g   Saturates 1.7g   Sugars 15.0g   Salt 0.3g

Fruit/Veg Portion 3

VEGETABLES RECIPES

Sweet Potato Soup

Servings: 2

Cooking Time: 25 Minutes

Ingredients:

- 1 tsp rapeseed oil
- 1 onion, chopped
- 2 cloves garlic, crushed
- 1 small carrot, chopped
- 450g sweet potato, peeled and chopped
- 450ml low-salt vegetable stock
- 2 tbsp fresh parsley, chopped
- freshly ground black pepper

Directions:

1. Heat the oil in a medium pan, add the onion and the garlic and fry for 3-4 minutes, until softened.

2. Add the carrot and the sweet potato and continue to fry for 2-3 minutes.

3. Pour over the stock, bring to the boil and simmer for 12-15 minutes until the vegetables are tender.

4. Transfer to a blender or food processor and blend until smooth.

5. Return to the pan, stir through the parsley, season well and serve with crusty bread.

Recipe Tips

Spice this up with 1 tsp curry paste or a pinch of chilli flakes.

Try adding chopped coriander in place of the parsley.

Freezing instructions: Freeze in portions then defrost in the fridge; or defrost in a microwave stirring regularly.

Nutrition:

KCal 294   Carbs 55.9g   Fibre 11.0g   Protein 4.1g

Fat 3.5g   Saturates 0.4g   Sugars 19.6g   Salt 0.51g

Fruit/Veg Portion 4

Summer Vegetables With Citrus Dressing

Servings: 4

Cooking Time: 3 Minutes

Ingredients:

- 100g fine beans, halved
- 3 baby courgettes/1 medium courgette, cut into chunks
- 150g broad beans, (shelled and skinned weight, or use frozen)
- 100g fresh/frozen peas
- 3 spring onions, sliced
- 2 tbsp coriander, chopped
- 1 tbsp pumpkin seeds, toasted
- 1 tsp olive oil
- grated zest and juice 1 lime

Directions:

1. Place the fine beans into a pan of boiling water and cook for 2 minutes.

2. Add the courgettes, broad beans and peas and

continue to cook for 1 minute. Drain and refresh under cold water, then transfer to a serving dish.

3. Mix together the remaining ingredients and toss through the vegetables. Serve.

Recipe Tips

To toast pumpkin seeds, add to a dry pan and fry over a medium heat for 2-3 minutes stirring regularly until they start to brown.

You could use lemon or orange in place of lime.

Nutrition:

KCal 102   Carbs 8.0g   Fibre 6.3g   Protein 6.4g   Fat 3.5g   Saturates 0.6g   Sugars 2.9g   Salt 0.02g Fruit/Veg Portion 1

Stuffed Parathas

Servings: 16

Cooking Time: 40 Minutes

Ingredients:

- For the filling:
- 1 large sweet potato (approx. 350g), peeled and quartered
- 4 spring onions, chopped
- 1 tsp ground turmeric
- 1 tsp ground cumin
- 1 tsp ground coriander
- 2 cloves garlic, crushed
- ½ red chilli, finely chopped
- 25g fresh coriander, chopped
- 50g frozen peas, defrosted
- For the dough:

- 200g wholemeal flour
- ½ tsp baking powder
- 100g 0% fat yogurt
- 125ml water
- 2 tsp rapeseed oil

Directions:

1. Boil the sweet potato for 10–15 minutes until soft, then drain and mash.

2. Add the spring onions, turmeric, cumin, ground coriander, garlic and chilli, fresh coriander and peas to the sweet potato. Mix well and reserve.

3. Add the flour to a bowl with the baking powder, yogurt and water. Mix well into a dough.

4. Divide the dough into 8 balls. On a lightly floured surface, roll each ball out into thin circles, creating 8 pancakes.

5. Divide the filling into four and spread it out over four of the dough circles, leaving a 1cm border around the edge.

6. Brush the edges with a little water, then place another dough circle on top, pressing the edges firmly together.

7. Brush a non-stick frying pan with ½ tsp oil, then place a paratha in the pan and cook over a low to medium heat for 2 minutes, turn over with a spatula and cook the other side for 2 minutes. Flip again and give each side one more minute. (When ready, the surface of the paratha should have a few brown spots). Repeat with the remaining parathas.

8. Cut into quarters to serve.

Recipe Tips

These parathas can be spiced up by adding some chopped fresh chilli and grated ginger when mixing the filling.

Nutrition:

KCal 78   Carbs 13.7g   Fibre 2.3g   Protein 2.8g   Fat 0.8g   Saturates 0.1g   Sugars 1.9g   Salt 0.07g   Fruit/Veg Portion 1

Stuffed Baby Peppers

Servings: 20

Cooking Time: 25-30 Minutes

Ingredients:

- 50g quinoa
- 1 clove garlic, crushed
- 10g raisins, roughly chopped
- 1 tsp ground cumin
- 1 spring onion, finely chopped
- 1 tbsp tomato puree
- juice half lemon
- 1 tsp oil
- 10 mixed baby peppers
- 5 cherry tomatoes, quartered
- 75g reduced-fat mozzarella, sliced into 10 pieces
- 1 tsp chopped chives, to garnish
- good grind black pepper

Directions:

1. Preheat the oven to 180°C/gas 4.
2. Rinse the quinoa in a sieve, then add to a pan with 150ml water. Bring to the boil, turn down the heat and simmer gently for 15 minutes. Drain off any unabsorbed water and fluff with a fork.
3. Place the quinoa in a bowl with the garlic, raisins, cumin, spring onion, tomato puree and lemon juice. Mix well and set aside.
4. Meanwhile, lightly oil a baking tray and halve the peppers lengthways, leaving the stems in place and removing the seeds.
5. Divide the quinoa evenly between the peppers and top each with a tomato quarter and a small piece of mozzarella.
6. Place the peppers onto a baking tray and bake for 10-12 minutes until the peppers have softened and the cheese has melted. Sprinkle with chives and a grind of black pepper.

Recipe Tips

You can assemble these the day before and leave in the fridge overnight and then bake them just before they are needed.

You could add other spices, such as curry powder, or use couscous instead of quinoa.

Freezing instructions: Freeze in portions then defrost in the microwave. Heat until piping-hot, stirring regularly. Eat immediately and discard any leftovers.

Nutrition:

KCal 23   Carbs 2.6g   Fibre 0.6g   Protein 1.3g   Fat 0.8g   Saturates 0.3g   Sugars 1.4g   Salt 0.03g   Fruit/Veg Portion 0

Strawberry Tart

Servings: 6

Cooking Time: 10 Minutes

Ingredients:

- 4 sheets filo pastry
- 2 tsp unsalted butter, melted
- 1 tbsp icing sugar
- 6 tbsp fat-free fromage frais
- 1 tbsp lemon curd
- 350g small ripe strawberries, hulled and sliced

Directions:

1. Preheat the oven to 200°C/gas 6. Set a sheet of filo pastry on a non-stick baking tray. Brush with a little melted butter and sprinkle with a little icing sugar.
2. Repeat three more times, reserving about 1 tsp of the icing sugar.
3. Bake for 10 minutes until golden. Leave to cool. Mix the fromage frais with the lemon curd and spread over the pastry.
4. Top with the strawberries and sprinkle with the reserved icing sugar. Serve immediately.

Recipe Tips

This also works well with raspberries.

If you don't have lemon curd, use 1 tbsp jam instead.

Nutrition:

KCal 136   Carbs 22.9g   Fibre 3.1g   Protein 3.7g   Fat 2.6g   Saturates 1.0g   Sugars 8.4g   Salt 0.25g

Stir-Fried Kale With Chilli, Ginger And Garlic

Servings: 4

Cooking Time: 8-9 Minutes

Ingredients:

- 2 tsp rapeseed oil
- 3cm fresh ginger root, peeled and finely chopped
- 2-3 cloves garlic, crushed
- pinch chilli flakes
- 200g curly kale, chopped (thick stalks removed)
- 4 tbsp water
- juice half lemon

Directions:

1. Add the oil to a pan over a low-medium heat and add the ginger and garlic, mixing well for 1–2 mins.
2. Now add the chilli flakes and stir for another minute.
3. Add the kale and mix well for 2–3 mins.
4. Turn the heat up, add the water, mix, put a lid on the pan and cook for a further 5–6 mins, stirring occasionally.
5. Drizzle with the lemon juice and serve.

Nutrition:

KCal 38   Carbs 1.3g   Fibre 2.2g   Protein 1.9g   Fat 2.3g   Saturates 0.2g   Sugars 0.9g   Salt 0.06g   Fruit/Veg Portion 0

Spinach And Wensleydale Stuffed Portobello Mushroom

Servings: 1

Cooking Time: 15 Minutes

Ingredients:

- 1 small onion, finely chopped
- 1 tsp olive oil
- 1 large portobello mushroom
- 100g baby spinach leaves
- good pinch dried thyme
- 1 clove garlic, crushed
- 1 tsp Dijon mustard
- 1 slice wholemeal bread, crumbled
- good pinch pepper
- 25g Wensleydale cheese, cut into small cubes (or Cheddar, feta or goat's cheese)

Directions:

1. Preheat the oven to 180°C/gas 4.
2. Add the onion to a pan with the oil and cook until well browned.
3. Remove the stalk from the mushroom, chop it up and add it to the onion, along with the spinach, thyme and garlic.
4. Once the spinach has wilted, add the mustard, bread and pepper, and mix well. Cover and leave for a couple of minutes so the bread absorbs all the flavours.
5. Mix the stuffing again and then pile it onto the mushroom cap.
6. Sprinkle the cheese evenly on top, pressing it into the stuffing, and bake for 10 minutes.

Recipe Tips

Frozen spinach is a useful ingredient to keep in your freezer. Look out for leaf spinach, rather than chopped, and always defrost it before using so that you can squeeze out the excess water.

Fresh spinach leaves are a great alternative to lettuce.

If you don't like Wensleydale, try adding the same amount of Cheddar, feta or goat's cheese.

Freezing instructions: Freeze with greaseproof paper between each mushroom. Defrost for 1 hour, then heat in the microwave or a moderate oven.

Nutrition:

KCal 289   Carbs 23.8g   Fibre 6.5g   Protein 15.7g

Fat 13.2g   Saturates 5.7g   Sugars 7.5g   Salt 1.1g

Fruit/Veg Portion 3

Spinach, Red Onion And Potato Tortilla

Servings: 4

Cooking Time: 45 Minutes

Ingredients:

- 400g new potatoes
- 250g frozen leaf spinach (130g once defrosted and excess water squeezed out)
- 1 tbsp olive oil
- 1 large red onion, thinly sliced
- 5 eggs
- pinch pepper, to season

Directions:

1. Boil the potatoes in their skins for 15–20 minutes (depending on size) until almost cooked, but still firm. Drain and run them under a cold tap to make them easier to handle, before cutting each potato into ½cm-thick slices.

2. Meanwhile, defrost the spinach, squeeze out the excess water and chop it slightly.

3. Add the oil to a large non-stick frying pan and put onto a medium heat. Add the onion and cook for 2–3 minutes until soft.

4. Beat the eggs with the pepper, mix in the spinach and then add the potatoes.

5. Pour the egg mixture into the frying pan. Use a spatula to press the tortilla down, and to press in the sides to create an even shape.

6. Once the tortilla has almost set (approx 5 minutes) invert onto a plate, then slide it back into the pan to cook the other side for 5 minutes. Reduce the heat and turn the tortilla twice more, cooking for 2–3 minutes on each side to make sure the centre is cooked.

7. Slide the tortilla onto a plate and leave to cool for 10-15 minutes. Ideally, serve warm, as it tastes much better. For a packed lunch, allow to cool completely before slicing and packing.

Recipe Tips

For this tortilla recipe (also known as Spanish omelette), you can use other vegetables instead of spinach, such as peas and red pepper. Or, try adding some herbs or garlic.

Nutrition:

KCal 233   Carbs 19.1g   Fibre 4.2g   Protein 13.8g   Fat 10.3g   Saturates 2.4g   Sugars 4.2g   Salt 0.33g   Fruit/Veg Portion 1

Spinach, Lemon And Feta Salad

Servings: 3

Cooking Time: 5 Minutes

Ingredients:

- 250g fresh spinach
- 1 tbsp pine nuts
- 30g feta cheese
- grated zest and juice 1 lemon
- 1 tbsp extra-virgin olive oil
- freshly ground black pepper

Directions:

1. Wash the spinach and add to a pan with a lid, cook

for 2-3 minutes stirring a couple of times (there is no need to add oil or extra water, there will be enough water clinging to the spinach after washing). Strain off excess water and allow to cool.

2. Meanwhile, add the pine nuts to a dry pan and stir regularly for 1-2 minutes until they are just starting to brown, remove from pan and reserve.

3. Gently squeeze out any remaining water from the spinach and distribute over a platter.

4. Crumble the feta cheese over the top, then scatter with the roasted pine nuts.

5. Sprinkle lemon zest over the dish, then drizzle with the lemon juice and olive oil. Season with pepper and serve.

Recipe Tips

You could try scattering this salad with a little goat's cheese or shavings of Parmesan cheese instead of feta. Or use lightly toasted flaked almonds or sunflower seeds rather than pine nuts.

This can be made in advance but only add the lemon juice and oil just before serving.

Also works with frozen spinach, just defrost and squeeze out the excess water, there is no need to cook it.

Nutrition:

KCal 119   Carbs 1.8g   Fibre 2.5g   Protein 4.7g   Fat 9.8g   Saturates 2.2g   Sugars 1.7g   Salt 0.54g Fruit/Veg Portion 1

Spinach, Corn And Chickpea Fritters

Servings: 4

Cooking Time: 20 Minutes

Ingredients:

- 2 tsp rapeseed oil
- 1 small onion, grated
- 1 red pepper, finely chopped
- 1 egg, beaten
- 150g frozen spinach, defrosted, water squeezed out, roughly chopped
- 1 tsp cumin
- 1 red chilli, finely chopped
- 80g frozen corn, defrosted
- 400g can chickpeas, drained and mashed thoroughly)
- 25g gram flour
- 10g fresh coriander, chopped
- salad, to serve

Directions:

1. Add 1 tsp of oil to a saucepan, then add the onion. Cook for 2-3 minutes, then add the red pepper and fry a further 4-5 minutes.

2. Meanwhile, add the egg, spinach, cumin, chilli and sweetcorn to a bowl and mix well.

3. Stir in the onion and red pepper, then add the chickpeas, gram flour and coriander, and mix thoroughly.With wet hands, shape the mixture into 8 patties.

4. Add the remaining oil to a large non-stick frying pan over a medium heat. Place fritters in the pan and flatten slightly with a spatula to about ½-1cm thick, to ensure even cooking.

5. Cook the fritters until lightly browned for 3-4 minutes, then carefully flip over and cook the other side again for 3-4 minutes. You may wish to give each side a further 1-2 minutes to get a nice crust on them. Serve with salad.

Recipe Tips

The nutritional information above does not include salad as a serving suggestion.

If you don't have a big enough pan, you can cook the fritters in two batches. Place on a warm plate and set aside until they're all ready.

You can serve the fritters either warm or cold.

If you don't have gram flour you could use plain or wholemeal wheat flour instead.

Freezing instructions: Freeze in individually wrapped portions with greaseproof paper between each fritter. Defrost thoroughly and reheat until piping hot throughout.

Nutrition:

KCal 181   Carbs 18.8g   Fibre 8.8g   Protein 10.7g

Fat 5.0g   Saturates 0.7g   Sugars 5.8g   Salt 0.74g

Fruit/Veg Portion 2

Spinach And Ricotta Cannelloni

Servings: 6

Cooking Time: 25 Minutes

Ingredients:

- 1 tsp rapeseed oil
- 1 large onion, finely chopped
- 1 leek, finely chopped
- 3 cloves garlic, crushed
- 250g frozen leaf spinach
- 150g ricotta cheese
- half tsp nutmeg
- 120g cannelloni (dry weight), cooked according to pack instructions and refreshed in cold water
- 400g can chopped tomatoes
- 1 heaped tsp oregano
- 1 tbsp tomato puree
- good grind black pepper
- 25g Mozzarella, thinly sliced

Directions:

1. Preheat the oven to 180°C/gas 4. Add the oil to a saucepan and cook the onion and leeks for 5-8 minutes. Mix in the garlic, cook together for 1 minute and remove from the heat.

2. Add the spinach, ricotta cheese and nutmeg and mix well.

3. Meanwhile, put the tomatoes in a bowl and add the oregano, tomato puree and pepper. Mix together to make the sauce.

4. Stuff the spinach and ricotta mixture into the cannelloni.

5. Put half the tomato sauce into an ovenproof dish. Place the stuffed cannelloni on top and add the remaining sauce. Top with Mozzarella and bake for 15 minutes.

Recipe Tips

Cooking pasta, draining and placing it immediately in cold water, stops it from continuing to cook and makes sure it doesn't go soggy.

For a dairy-free/vegan alternative, use soft tofu in place of the ricotta and top with a little dairy-free or vegan alternative to cheese.

Nutrition:

KCal 171   Carbs 20.8g   Fibre 4.2g   Protein 8.5g   Fat 5.0g   Saturates 2.4g   Sugars 6.1g   Salt 0.14g   Fruit/Veg Portion 2

Spinach And Rice Soup

Servings: 2

Cooking Time: 40 Minutes

Ingredients:

- 1 tsp rapeseed oil
- 1 small onion, chopped
- 1 clove garlic, crushed
- 1 carrot, finely chopped
- 100g brown rice
- 150g bag fresh or frozen spinach
- 900ml low-salt vegetable stock
- 2 tbsp single cream
- freshly ground black pepper

Directions:

1. Heat the oil in a medium frying pan.
2. Add the onion, garlic and carrot and fry for 3–4 minutes until beginning to soften.
3. Stir in the rice, spinach and stock, bring to the boil and simmer gently for 35 minutes until the rice is tender. Transfer to a blender or food processor with the cream and plenty of black pepper, blitz until smooth then return to the pan to reheat.

Recipe Tips

If using frozen spinach in place of fresh, you'll only need 100g.

If you don't use the soup straight away, you may need to add extra stock or water when you reheat as it will thicken after a while.

Freezing instructions: Freeze in portions then defrost in the microwave. Heat until piping-hot, stirring regularly. Eat immediately and discard any leftovers.

Nutrition:

KCal 310   Carbs 49.1g   Fibre 6.4g   Protein 7.6g   Fat 7.8g   Saturates 2.2g   Sugars 8.7g   Salt 0.87g   Fruit/Veg Portion 2

Spinach And Mushroom Lasagne

Servings: 6

Cooking Time: 45 Minutes

Ingredients:

- 800g tin chopped tomatoes
- 1 tbsp tomato puree
- 2 cloves garlic, crushed
- 1 heaped tsp dried oregano
- 1 tsp olive oil
- 1 onion, finely chopped
- 1 large red pepper, finely chopped
- 250g mushrooms, thinly sliced
- 2 tsp plain flour
- 250ml skimmed milk
- 300g frozen spinach (150g when defrosted and drained)
- 100g extra-light cream cheese
- 1 tsp Dijon mustard
- good pinch black pepper
- 250g pack wholemeal lasagne
- 2-3 fresh tomatoes, thinly sliced
- 30g Cheddar
- 6 fresh, torn basil leaves, to garnish

Directions:

1. Preheat the oven to 180°C/gas 4. Blend together the tomatoes, tomato puree, garlic and oregano to make a tomato sauce, then set aside.

2. Heat the oil in a pan and add the onion. Cook for 2–3 minutes, add the red pepper and cook a further 2–3 minutes. Add the mushrooms, cook for 2 minutes then gradually stir in the flour to coat the vegetables.

3. Gradually, stir in the milk until it starts to thicken, add the spinach and stir for 1 minute then stir in the cream cheese, mustard and black pepper.

4. To an ovenproof dish add a little of the tomato sauce then top with a layer of lasagne. Now add a layer of the mushroom, spinach and cheese mix and repeat until you end with a layer of tomato sauce then top with the thinly sliced tomatoes.

5. Sprinkle with Cheddar and bake for 30–35 minutes. Scatter with fresh basil to serve.

Recipe Tips

For a gluten-free version or if you're watching your carb intake, use 3-4 sliced aubergines in place of the lasagne sheets and use gluten-free flour in the sauce.

Freezing instructions: Suitable for freezing once cooked. Defrost in the fridge or microwave and reheat until piping-hot throughout.

Nutrition:

KCal 287   Carbs 40.0g   Fibre 9.1g   Protein 15.3g

Fat 5.0g   Saturates 1.9g   Sugars 12.8g   Salt 0.41g

Fruit/Veg Portion 3

Spicy Roasted Chickpeas

Servings: 4

Cooking Time: 25-30 Minutes

Ingredients:

- 400g tin chickpeas
- 2 tsp rapeseed oil
- half tsp ground cumin
- half tsp chilli powder

Directions:

1. Drain and rinse the chickpeas, and pat dry with kitchen paper.

2. Preheat the oven to 190°C/gas 5. Oil a large baking tray with 1 tsp rapeseed oil and place the tray in the oven for 3 minutes.

3. Spread the chickpeas onto the hot baking tray and cook for 15 minutes, mixing a couple of times to make sure they cook evenly.

4. Remove from the oven, place the chickpeas in a bowl and drizzle with the remaining oil. Mix well. Add the cumin and chilli powder. Mix again and tip back onto the baking tray.

5. Roast for another 10-15 minutes until brown and crunchy.

6. Serve immediately or enjoy cool.

Recipe Tips

These can be made the day before and stored in an airtight container. If you'd like to serve them warm just reheat in a hot oven for two minutes.

This snack counts as half a portion of fruit and veg.

Nutrition:

KCal 79   Carbs 8.1g   Fibre 2.9g   Protein 3.9g   Fat 2.9g   Saturates 0.2g   Sugars 0.4g   Salt 0.4g   Fruit/Veg Portion 0

Spicy Butternut Squash Soup

Servings: 4

Cooking Time: 30-40 Minutes

Ingredients:

- 1 tbsp rapeseed oil
- 1 onion, chopped
- half–1 red chilli, chopped
- 1 clove garlic, crushed
- 2x medium butternut squash, peeled, deseeded and chopped
- 1 tbsp medium curry paste
- 1 low-salt vegetable stock cube
- 200ml reduced-fat coconut milk
- 2 tbsp fresh coriander, chopped
- freshly ground black pepper, to serve
- slice chilli and coriander leaves, to garnish

Directions:

1. Heat the oil in a saucepan. Add the onion, chilli and garlic, and fry for 4-5 minutes until softened.

2. Add the squash and continue to fry for 5 minutes. Stir in the curry paste and fry for a further minute.

3. Pour 500ml boiling water over the squash, crumble in the stock cube and bring to the boil. Cover and simmer for 15-20 minutes, until the squash is tender. Transfer to a food processor or blender and blend until smooth.

4. Return to the pan, add the coconut milk and coriander. Heat through and serve sprinkled with black pepper. Garnish with a slice of chilli and torn coriander leaves.

Recipe Tips

If you don't like things too spicy, omit the chilli and use a mild curry paste or powder instead.

You could make this soup with sweet potato instead of butternut squash.

Freezing instructions: Freeze in portions then defrost in the fridge, or defrost in a microwave taking care to stir regularly.

Nutrition:

KCal 204   Carbs 25.3g   Fibre 6.6g   Protein 3.9g   Fat 8.2g   Saturates 3.4g   Sugars 14.2g   Salt 0.3g Fruit/Veg Portion 3

Spicy Bean Quesadillas

Servings: 2

Cooking Time: 10 Minutes

Ingredients:

- 2 wholemeal tortillas
- 1 tbsp almond butter
- half tin pinto beans, roughly mashed
- 1 tbsp tomato puree
- 80g frozen peas, defrosted and roughly mashed
- half tsp ground cumin
- half tsp oregano
- half tsp mild chilli powder
- 2 spring onions, finely chopped
- 1 tomato, finely chopped
- half green pepper, finely chopped
- 1 tbsp fresh coriander, roughly chopped, plus a little to serve
- 1 tbsp finely chopped red onion, to serve

Directions:

1. Spread the tortillas lightly with nut butter.
2. Mix everything else apart from the red onion together, and spread over one tortilla, laying the other tortilla on top.
3. Cook in a non-stick pan over a low heat (no need for oil) until the tortilla is turning browned and crisp.
4. Turn the tortilla over and cook the other side (3-5 minutes each side).
5. Place on a board and slice, then scatter with red onion and coriander. Serve with salad.

Recipe Tips

You can make up the tortillas in advance and fry when ready to eat.

Nutrition:

KCal 371   Carbs 49.9g   Fibre 12.9g   Protein 17.0g Fat 8.6g   Saturates 2.0g   Sugars 7.5g   Salt 0.7g Fruit/Veg Portion 2

Spicy Potato Wedges

Servings: 8

Cooking Time: 30 Minutes

Ingredients:

- 8 baking potatoes, each cut into 8 wedges (total weight 1.6kg)
- 3 tbsp rapeseed oil
- 1 tbsp paprika
- For the garlic and herb dip:
- 200g tub half-fat cream cheese
- 200g pot fat-free fromage frais
- 2 cloves garlic, crushed
- 3 tbsp fresh mint, chopped
- 3 tbsp fresh parsley, chopped
- For the spicy tomato salsa:
- 400g tin chopped tomatoes
- 1 red chilli
- 1 clove garlic, crushed
- 3 tbsp fresh coriander, chopped

Directions:

1. Preheat the oven to 200°C/gas 6.
2. Place the potato wedges in a large pan of boiling water and simmer for 5 minutes. Drain and place in a large roasting tin.
3. Mix together the oil and the paprika and toss through the potato wedges. Place on a baking tray and cook for 20-25 minutes until golden and crisp.
4. For the garlic and herb dip, simply combine all the ingredients and spoon into a serving dish.
5. Drain any excess liquid from the tomatoes then blend with the chilli, garlic and coriander for 30 seconds. Spoon into a serving dish.
6. Serve the potatoes with the dips.

Recipe Tips

If you're passing these around as finger food, omit the paprika from the potatoes as it stains the fingers!

You could use Chinese 5 Spice powder in place of paprika, or try dried thyme.

Freezing instructions: Wedges are suitable for freezing. Defrost in the microwave and reheat in the oven until piping hot.

Nutrition:

KCal 278   Carbs 41.6g   Fibre 5.0g   Protein 9.2g   Fat 7.2g   Saturates 2.3g   Sugars 5.5g   Salt 0.15g   Fruit/Veg Portion 0

Spiced Red Cabbage

Servings: 8

Cooking Time: 45 Minutes

Ingredients:

- 1kg red cabbage, cored and finely sliced
- 2 eating apples, sliced
- 1 cinnamon stick
- 8 cloves
- 1 tbsp light soft brown sugar
- 2 tbsp white wine vinegar
- knob of butter

Directions:

1. Place all the ingredients into a large pan with a tight fitting lid.

2. Cover and cook over a low heat for 45 minutes, stirring occasionally, until the cabbage is tender. Serve.

Recipe Tips

Adding vinegar to red cabbage while it is cooking, helps it keep its colour.

You could add raisins and/or walnuts to the cabbage when almost ready.

You can also use raw red cabbage to make a really colourful coleslaw.

Nutrition:

KCal 67   Carbs 10.4g   Fibre 4.1g   Protein 1.6g   Fat 1.1g   Saturates 0.4g   Sugars 10.0g   Salt 0.04g   Fruit/Veg Portion 2

Spanish Onion And Anchovy Pizza

Servings: 8

Cooking Time: 30-35 Minutes

Ingredients:

- 200g strong plain flour
- quarter tsp salt
- 7g sachet easy-blend yeast
- 2 tbsp olive oil
- 75ml semi-skimmed milk
- 2 large onions, finely sliced
- 25g tin anchovies, drained and roughly chopped
- 1 tbsp pinenuts
- 1 tbsp sultanas
- half tsp chilli flakes
- 2 tsp fresh chives, chopped, to garnish

Directions:

Preheat the oven to 200°C/gas 6. In a large bowl, sift together the flour and salt. Stir through the yeast. Mix together half of the oil, the milk and 50ml hand hot water, pour into the flour and combine to form a dough. Tip the dough out onto a lightly floured surface and knead for 5 minutes until smooth.

Place in a lightly oiled bowl, cover with a damp cloth and set aside in a warm place for 1 hour until doubled in size. Re-knead, then shape into a square approximately 40cm x 40cm.

Meanwhile, heat the remaining oil in a frying pan, add the onions and fry gently for 8–10 minutes until softened and beginning to turn golden.

Scatter over the pizza base along with the remaining ingredients except chives, then bake for 20–25 minutes until the pizza base is golden and crisp. Scatter with the chives and serve.

Recipe Tips

For a vegetarian version, use 75g shredded sundried tomatoes in place of the anchovies.

Make the pizza with red onions for more colour.

Nutrition:

KCal 168   Carbs 24.4g   Fibre 2.1g   Protein 5.5g   Fat 4.9g   Saturates 0.7g   Sugars 4.8g   Salt 0.62g   Fruit/Veg Portion 0

Spaetzle

Servings: 4

Cooking Time: 15 Minutes

Ingredients:

- 250g plain flour
- 1 large egg, beaten
- pinch nutmeg
- 2 tsp olive oil
- 1 tbsp fresh parsley, chopped

Directions:

1. Bring a large saucepan of water to the boil.
2. In a large bowl, stir together the flour, egg and nutmeg. Gradually stir in approx 100ml cold water to make a smooth dough that doesn't stick to the spoon.
3. Flour a cutting board, place the dough on it and roll out thinly. Cut the dough into small noodles about 5cm long. Cook the noodles in batches by adding to the boiling water. They cook quickly and are ready when they float to the surface. As the noodles finish cooking, remove them with a slotted spoon.
4. Transfer the noodles to a plate and toss with the olive oil and some parsley.

Recipe Tips

Try making spaetzle with half wholemeal flour for more fibre.

For a simple sauce for 2, sauté a large chopped leek with 150g mushrooms. Stir in 2 tbsp reduced fat garlic and herb cream cheese.

Nutrition:

KCal 270   Carbs 48.3g   Fibre 2.8g   Protein 8.6g

Fat 4.1g   Saturates 1.0g   Sugars 0.5g   Salt 0.39g

Fruit/Veg Portion 0

Soda Bread Pizzetta

Servings: 8

Cooking Time: 10 minutesr

Ingredients:

- 2 fresh tomatoes, thinly sliced
- 1 red onion, very thinly sliced
- 100g sweetcorn
- 50g reduced-fat mozzarella, sliced thinly
- 125g wholemeal flour and sprinkle for rolling
- half tsp bicarbonate of soda
- 1 tbsp yogurt
- 1 tsp rapeseed oil
- 1 tbsp tomato puree
- 1 heaped tsp oregano

Directions:

1. Preheat the oven to 190°C/gas 5. Prepare all the vegetables and slice the cheese for the toppings.
2. Add the flour and bicarbonate of soda to a mixing bowl.
3. Thoroughly mix in the yogurt and 75ml water. Shape into eight small balls and roll into rounds, using a little flour to stop them sticking.
4. Place on a lightly oiled baking sheet and spread with tomato puree then add a slice of tomato, sprinkle with oregano. Scatter with onion and sweetcorn and top each with a slice of mozzarella.

5. Bake for 10 minutes and serve.

Recipe Tips

You could use any toppings you like – try spinach, red pepper and onion, or use reduced-fat Cheddar instead of mozzarella.

Make each pizzetta half the size for perfect party nibbles.

Freezing instructions: Suitable for freezing once cooked. Freeze with greaseproof paper between each pizetta. Defrost 1 hour then bake as normal.

Nutrition:

KCal 99   Carbs 16.9g   Fibre 2.9g   Protein 3.3g   Fat 1.3g   Saturates 0.2g   Sugars 2.7g   Salt 0.24g Fruit/Veg Portion 0

Soda Bread

Servings: 8

Cooking Time: 25–30 Minutes

Ingredients:

- 250g wholemeal plain flour
- 200g plain flour
- half tsp bicarbonate of soda
- half tsp cream of tartar
- 25g butter
- 300ml buttermilk

Directions:

1. Sift together the flours, bicarbonate of soda and cream of tartar into a bowl and rub in the butter until the mixture resembles fine breadcrumbs. Quickly stir in the buttermilk and combine until a dough is formed.

2. Turn the dough onto a lightly floured surface and knead until smooth. Mould into a round shape, place onto a lightly floured baking sheet, cut a cross in the top, and sprinkle with a little flour.

3. Preheat the oven to 180°C/gas 5 and bake for 25–30 minutes, until it sounds hollow when tapped.

Recipe Tips

When sieving wholemeal flour, add back any bran that stays in the sieve after sifting.

You could add 75g mixed dried fruit and 1 tsp of mixed spice for a great fruit bread.

This soda bread is ideal for slicing and freezing – pop the slices straight into the toaster.

Freezing instructions: Suitable for freezing once cooked. Slice, then wrap in foil to freeze. You can then use slices as required.

Nutrition:

KCal 240   Carbs 41.9g   Fibre 4.2g   Protein 7.6g   Fat 3.7g   Saturates 1.9g   Sugars 2.4g   Salt 0.28g Fruit/Veg Portion 0

Smoky Tofu Kebabs

Servings: 4

Cooking Time: 10–15 Minutes

Ingredients:

- 200g pack firm tofu, drained
- 2–3 medium courgettes, sliced thinly lengthways into 12 slices (300g)
- For the marinade:
- 2 tbsp toasted coriander seeds
- 1 tbsp toasted cumin seeds
- 4 cloves garlic, peeled
- 4cm piece ginger, roughly chopped
- 2 red chillies, deseeded and roughly chopped
- freshly ground black pepper
- 1 tbsp sundried tomato purée
- 3 tbsp white wine vinegar
- 3 tbsp extra-virgin olive oil
- 2 tbsp water

Directions:

1. Drain the tofu well and cut into 12 large cubes.
2. To make the marinade, begin by grinding the coriander and cumin seeds to a powder.
3. Next, pound the garlic, ginger and chillies with a couple of big pinches of pepper, to a rough paste in a mortar. Now work in the coriander and cumin, tomato purée, vinegar, and olive oil, then mix in 2 tbsp water.
4. Add the tofu to the marinade and mix gently, cover and set aside for a minimum of an hour, preferably 3–4 hours or longer. Microwave the courgette slices in two batches, covered in clingfilm, for about 60–80 seconds, until just tender enough to wrap around a piece of tofu but not so soft that they collapse. Alternatively, blanch in boiling water for 30 seconds or so and drain well.
5. Shortly before cooking, wrap strips of courgette around the cubes of tofu and slide onto skewers, so that the courgette stays in place.
6. Brush the courgette with any marinade left in the bowl, and grill or barbecue for 10-15 minutes, turning regularly.

Nutrition:

KCal 176   Carbs 3.2g   Fibre 4.0g   Protein 9.0g   Fat 13.2g   Saturates 1.9g   Sugars 2.3g   Salt 0.04g   Fruit/Veg Portion 0

Smoky Roast Vegetables With Sesame Yogurt

Servings: 3

Cooking Time: 45 Minutes

Ingredients:

- 1 carrot, cut into chunks
- 200g Jerusalem artichokes, cut into chunks
- 1 sweet potato, cut into chunks
- 2 red onions, quartered
- 2 peppers – red and green, quartered
- 1 tbsp olive oil
- 2 heaped tsp mild (dulce) smoked paprika
- For the sesame yogurt:
- 2 tsp tahini

- 4 tbsp 0% fat Greek yogurt

Directions:

1. Add the carrot, artichokes, sweet potato, onions and peppers to a large bowl with the oil and mix well.

2. Add the paprika and mix again, so all vegetables are coated.

3. Spread out onto a lightly oiled baking sheet and bake in a preheated oven at 180°C/gas 4 for 35–45 minutes, turning occasionally.

4. Meanwhile, mix the tahini with the yogurt and reserve until the vegetables are ready.

Recipe Tips

Use a plant-based yogurt alternative to make this dish vegan.

Serve with chickpeas and wholemeal pitta bread or rice to turn this into a meal.

Nutrition:

KCal 271   Carbs 34.6g   Fibre 12.1g   Protein 7.7g   Fat 2.7g   Saturates 1.3g   Sugars 16.8g   Salt 0.15g Fruit/Veg Portion 2

Cheddar And Leek Pancakes

Servings: 4

Cooking Time: 10-15 Minutes

Ingredients:

- 2 tsp rapeseed oil
- 1 leek, finely chopped
- 1 egg, beaten
- 150ml semi-skimmed milk
- 100g wholemeal flour
- 50g reduced-fat mature Cheddar cheese, finely diced
- pinch pepper

Directions:

1. Add 1 tsp of the oil to a saucepan over a low to medium heat, then add the leek. Cook for 3–4 minutes, stirring regularly until the leek has softened, then remove from the heat.

2. Beat the egg into the milk, then place the flour in a bowl and gradually stir in the milk mixture until smooth. Next, add the cheese and leek. Mix well. Season with the pepper.

3. Heat a non-stick pan. Add the remaining oil and wipe it around the pan with kitchen paper, then add 1 tbsp of the mixture.

4. Cook for 2 minutes, then flip over with a spatula and cook for another minute or two on the other side. The pancakes should be about 8cm in diameter and only 3–4mm thick. You should be able to cook 2 or 3 in a large pan at the same time.

Recipe Tips

The ingredients should be finely chopped to ensure even cooking.

For extra flavour, add fresh herbs, such as chives, basil or tarragon.

Nutrition:

KCal 201   Carbs 19.7g   Fibre 4.0g   Protein 11.1g   Fat 7.7g   Saturates 2.3g   Sugars 3.1g   Salt 0.31g   Fruit/Veg Portion 0

Slow-Roasted Garlic And Herb Tomatoes

Servings: 2

Cooking Time: 1 Hour

Ingredients:

- 6 cloves garlic, crushed
- 1 tsp dried oregano
- 2 pinches ground black pepper
- 1 tbsp olive oil, plus a little extra to oil a baking tray
- 4 large vine tomatoes (approx. 500g)

Directions:

1. Preheat the oven to 150°C/ gas 2. Mix the garlic, oregano, pepper and olive oil, crushing it all together with the back of a spoon.
2. Cut the tomatoes in half through the middle (equator). Then - with the tomatoes cut side up - make a few cuts into the centre of each half, being careful not to pierce through to the skin.
3. Divide the garlic mixture between the tomatoes, gently pushing it into the flesh.

4. Place on a lightly oiled baking sheet and bake in the oven for 1 hour.

Recipe Tips

These tomatoes will keep in the fridge for up to two days and can be reheated when needed.

This dish is fantastic served on toasted ciabatta, or with grilled meat or fish.

Nutrition:

KCal 107   Carbs 8.5g   Fibre 3.6g   Protein 2.1g   Fat 6.4g   Saturates 1.0g   Sugars 7.3g   Salt 0.01g   Fruit/Veg Portion 1

Shakshuka

Servings: 1

Cooking Time: 20 Minutes

Ingredients:

- 1 small onion, finely sliced, approx 60g, unpeeled
- 1 red and 1 orange pepper, halved, deseeded and chopped, approx 120g unprepared weight
- 1 clove garlic, crushed
- 1tsp sundried tomato paste or tomato purée
- 1tsp smoked paprika
- 1/2tsp ground cumin
- 1/2tsp ground coriander
- 400g can chopped tomatoes
- 1 egg
- Fresh chopped parsley and mint

Directions:

1. Put the onion, peppers and garlic in a glass bowl

with 1tbsp water. Cover with cling film and microwave at 800W for 2 mins. Stir and cook for a further 2 mins.

2. Stir the paste and spices into the onion mixture and microwave for a further 1 min. Tip into a medium frying pan.

3. Stir in the tomatoes and simmer gently for 15 mins or until thickened, stirring occasionally.

4. Make a dip in the middle, crack the egg into the dip. Cover the pan with a lid and cook until the egg is done to your taste.

5. Scatter with red pepper flakes (optional), a little chopped parsley and mint, and serve.

Recipe Tips

You could use any colour peppers for this dish.

Try adding mushrooms or artichoke hearts.

Freezing instructions: the sauce can be frozen.

Nutrition:

KCal 259   Carbs 27.5g   Fibre 9.6g   Protein 16.7g

Fat 7.0g   Saturates 1.6g   Sugars 25.9g   Salt 0.3g

Fruit/Veg Portion 5

Scary Pumpkin Soup With Tombstone Bread

Servings: 4

Cooking Time: 30 Minutes

Ingredients:

- 2 tsp rapeseed oil
- 1 large onion, chopped
- 1 small butternut squash (500g prepared weight), peeled and cut into cubes
- 1 very low salt vegetable stock cube in 800ml boiling water
- 75g red lentils
- 400g can tomatoes
- 1 tbsp tomato puree
- good pinch pepper
- 4 slices wholemeal bread

Directions:

1. Add the onion to the pan with 1 teaspoon of oil. Cook gently until the onion starts to brown.

2. Now add the squash, stock, lentils, tomatoes and puree, and simmer for 15-20 minutes.

3. Add a good pinch of pepper, then whizz with a stick blender or in a food processor until smooth.

4. Meanwhile, cut the bread into the shape of a tombstone, put the stencil into position, and spray onto the toasted bread.

5. Put the soup into bowls. Add the yoghurt to a piping bag with a really small nozzle, and pipe a thin spiral onto the soup. Take a skewer or chopstick and draw

through the spiral from the centre outwards to create a spider's web. Add the toast and serve.

Recipe Tips

You could use an oat or soya-based, non-dairy alternative to yogurt for a lactose-free version.

The serving suggestion above includes wholemeal bread, but does not include the yogurt. For a lower-carb option, serve without bread.

Nutrition:

KCal 272   Carbs 44.6g   Fibre 8.5g   Protein 11.5g   Fat 3.3g   Saturates 0.3g   Sugars 14.5g   Salt 0.56g   Fruit/Veg Portion 4

Savoy Coleslaw

Servings: 8

Cooking Time: 1 hour

Ingredients:

- half Savoy cabbage (about 400g)
- 1 leek (100g)
- 2–3 carrots (200g)
- 3 tbsp extra-virgin olive oil
- juice 1 lemon
- 1 heaped tsp grain mustard
- pinch pepper

Directions:

1. Remove any really thick stems, then finely shred the cabbage using a mandolin or food processor.
2. Finely shred the leek and grate the carrots.
3. Add the olive oil, lemon juice, mustard and pepper. Mix well and refrigerate for at least and hour before

serving.

Nutrition:

KCal 68   Carbs 3.9g   Fibre 3.0g   Protein 1.4g   Fat 4.5g   Saturates 0.6g   Sugars 3.8g   Salt 0.09g   Fruit/Veg Portion 0

Savoury Popcorn

Servings: 6

Cooking Time: 10-15 Minutes

Ingredients:

- 60g popping corn (divided into two, 30g portions)
- For the cheesy garlic popcorn topping:
- 1 tsp rapeseed oil1-2 cloves garlic, crushed
- 1 tsp chopped fresh oregano (or half tsp dried)
- good grind pepper
- 10g Parmesan, very finely grated
- For the chilli lemon popcorn topping:
- 1 tsp rapeseed oil
- half red chilli, very finely chopped
- juice and finely grated zest 1 lemon
- 1 tsp chopped fresh thyme (or half tsp dried)

Directions:

1. Heat a large deep pan with a lid and place in the popping corn and cover. Shake the pan regularly and after 2-3 minutes you'll hear the corn start to pop – don't be tempted to open the lid. Keep shaking until the popping stops.
2. Put the popped-corn into a large bowl and discard any corn that hasn't popped. Repeat until all your

corn is done, then divide into two.

3. Meanwhile, make your flavourings. To make the cheesy garlic popcorn, add the oil to a pan with the garlic, oregano and pepper. Cook gently for 1 minute without browning the garlic. Add half the popped corn and the finely grated Parmesan. Mix well and serve.

4. To make the chilli lemon popcorn, add 1 tsp rapeseed oil to a pan with the red chilli. Cook gently for 1 minute.

5. Add the lemon juice and zest and heat a further minute until the lemon juice has halved in volume. Add the remaining half of popped corn, mix well and serve.

Recipe Tips

Don't put too much corn in at once – cook in batches as it expands a lot.

There's no end to the range of flavours you can make – try different spices such as cumin or smoked paprika. Just make sure you don't make the mix too wet or you'll get soggy popcorn.

Nutrition:

KCal 58   Carbs 7.7g   Fibre 0.5g   Protein 2.0g   Fat 2.0g   Saturates 0.4g   Sugars 0.2g   Salt 0.03g Fruit/Veg Portion 0

Saag Aloo (Spinach And Potatoes)

Servings: 6

Cooking Time: 50 Minutes

Ingredients:

- 1 tbsp olive oil
- 1 large onion, finely chopped
- 4 cloves garlic, finely chopped
- 1-3 green chillies (depending on how hot you like it), finely chopped
- 1 tbsp chopped fresh ginger
- 1 tsp turmeric
- 750g potatoes, peeled and cut into small pieces
- half-1.5 tsp red chilli powder
- 750g spinach leaves, washed and chopped

Directions:

1. Heat the oil in a non-stick frying pan, add the onion, garlic, chilli and ginger and cook for 2-3 minutes until softened.

2. Stir in the turmeric and cook for 5 minutes. Add the potatoes and red chilli powder, stir, cover and cook for 15-20 minutes over a medium heat, stirring regularly.

3. Stir through the spinach, cover and cook for 25 to 30 minutes, until the potatoes are tender and the mixture quite dry.

Recipe Tips

This dish works well with frozen spinach. Just defrost and add when the potatoes are almost cooked.

If you don't have fresh chillies, ginger or the spices you could add 1 tbsp curry paste – mild or hot, whichever you prefer.

Freezing instructions: Suitable for freezing once cooked. Defrost thoroughly and reheat until piping hot.

Nutrition:

KCal 180   Carbs 28.1g   Fibre 6.9g   Protein 6.5g   Fat 3.1g   Saturates 0.4g   Sugars 4.9g   Salt 0.47g Fruit/Veg Portion 1

Sage, Onion And Sweet Potato Stuffing

Servings: 6

Cooking Time: 30 Minutes

Ingredients:

- 2 large onions, roughly chopped
- 2 tsp rapseed oil
- pinch pepper
- 1 tsp dried sage
- 1 slice wholemeal bread, in breadcrumbs
- 100g mashed sweet potato

Directions:

1. Add the onions to a pan with the rapeseed oil and cook gently for 6–7 minutes until softened and starting to brown.

2. Add the pepper and sage. Then add the breadcrumbs, sweet potato and 200ml water from the boiled potato.

3. Mix well, place the mixture in a lightly oiled ovenproof dish and bake for 20 minutes until the top has browned.

Recipe Tips

If you don't like sage, try adding a tablespoon of freshly chopped parsley and a teaspoon of dried thyme or use oregano or tarragon instead.

Freezing instructions: Freeze in portions then defrost in the fridge,or defrost in a microwave and reheat until piping hot.

Nutrition:

KCal 65   Carbs 10.8g   Fibre 2.4g   Protein 1.5g   Fat 1.3g   Saturates 0.1g   Sugars 5.9g   Salt 0.08g Fruit/Veg Portion 0

Rosemary Baked Onions

Servings: 4

Cooking Time: 45 Minutes

Ingredients:

- 4 large onions
- 1 tbsp balsamic vinegar
- 4 tsp olive oil
- 4 cloves garlic
- sprigs rosemary
- good grind black pepper

Directions:

1. Preheat the oven to 180°C/gas 5. Remove the papery outer layer of the onions, leaving their skins intact, then trim off their tops and bottoms.

2. Cut a cross in the top of each onion, slicing down to cut into four, but only three quarters of the way through, making sure the onions stay whole.

3. Place each onion on a square of foil and create a loose parcel that's open at the top. Cut 4 cloves garlic

into 5 slices each, then push one slice into each of the cross cuts and one in the centre, pushing down to the core.

4. Do the same with the rosemary spigs, using one for each onion, breakingthe sprigs into smaller pieces.

5. Add balsamic vinegar, olive oil and a grind of pepper to each parcel. Then, bring up the corners of the foil and twist it at the top to seal. Bake for 45 minutes.

Recipe Tips

Open up the foil parcel at the table to enjoy the aromas that are sealed in.

Use smaller onions, but reduce the cooking time by 10 minutes.

Use fresh sprigs of thyme or sage as an alternative to rosemary.

Nutrition:

KCal 113   Carbs 16.6g   Fibre 4.6g   Protein 2.2g   Fat 3.2g   Saturates 0.4g   Sugars 12.7g   Salt 0.02g Fruit/Veg Portion 2

Roasted Vegetable Pizza

Servings: 4

Cooking Time: 35 Minutes

Ingredients:

- 75g potatoes, peeled and chopped small
- 50g gram (chickpea) flour
- 125g ground rice
- 50g cornflour
- half tsp bicarbonate of soda
- half tsp cream of tartar
- 25g sunflower spread
- 125ml semi-skimmed milk
- a little oil for greasing
- For the topping:
- 4 medium tomatoes, sliced
- half red pepper, sliced
- half yellow pepper, sliced
- 1 small red onion, sliced
- 1 small tin (290g) button mushrooms, drained and halved
- 40g feta cheese, crumbled
- handful fresh basil leaves, torn

Directions:

1. Add the potatoes to a pan of boiling water and cook 15 mins until soft, then mash.

2. Preheat the oven to 220ºC/gas 7. In a large bowl, mix together the gram flour, ground rice, cornflour, bicarbonate of soda and cream of tartar.

3. Rub in the potato and spread , until the mixture resembles breadcrumbs.

4. Add enough milk to make a soft dough and form into a ball, then roll out to a 30cm round and place on a lightly oiled baking sheet.

5. Top with slices of tomato, peppers and onion, and mushroom halves.

6. Crumble over the feta and bake for 15–20 minutes until the vegetables are tender and the pizza base is golden and crisp.

7. Scatter over the basil and serve.

Recipe Tips

To make a garlic crust, simply add 2-3 cloves crushed garlic to the potato.

For extra flavour, sprinkle 1 tsp dried organo and pinch of chilli flakes over the tomato slices before adding the peppers and onion.

Nutrition:

KCal 333   Carbs 52.3g   Fibre 5.3g   Protein 11.1g   Fat 7.7g   Saturates 3.0g   Sugars 7.2g   Salt 1.07g Fruit/Veg Portion 3

Roasted Red Vegetables With Ginger And Garlic

Servings: 8

Cooking Time: 45 Minutes

Ingredients:

- 2 tbsp extra-virgin olive oil
- 12 plum tomatoes, cut in half (stem to tip)
- 4 red peppers, deseeded, cut into eighths
- 3 red onions, quartered
- 5cm piece root ginger, peeled and chopped
- 12 cloves garlic (unpeeled)
- 4 big sprigs thyme
- freshly ground black pepper

Directions:

1. Preheat the oven to 200ºC/gas 6.

2. Add half the oil to a large, shallow ovenproof dish and pack in the tomatoes, peppers and onions into a single close layer.

3. Sprinkle with ginger and tuck garlic cloves and sprigs of thyme among them.

4. Drizzle over the remaining oil and season with pepper.

5. Turn so that everything is evenly coated then slide into the oven, uncovered.

6. Roast for about 40–45 minutes, turning occasionally, until tender and patched with brown. Serve hot or warm.

Recipe Tips

Once cooked, you can easily squeeze the garlic out of its

skin by pressing between your thumb and forefinger.

Turn this into a pasta sauce by roughly chopping the finished dish and stirring through cooked pasta.

Freezing instructions: Freeze in a bag. Defrost in a microwave and use as a sauce for pasta.

Nutrition:

KCal 106   Carbs 14.5g   Fibre 1.7g   Protein 2.4g   Fat 3.2g   Saturates 0.5g   Sugars 11.8g   Salt 0.02g Fruit/Veg Portion 3

Chargrilled Red Pepper And Tomato Salsa

Servings: 6

Cooking Time: 30 Minutes

Ingredients:

- 3 red peppers, deseeded and quartered
- 2 red onions, cut into wedges
- 200g ripe tomatoes, chopped
- 1 heaped tbsp tomato puree
- 1 tsp ground cumin
- 1 tsp oregano
- pinch chilli flakes (or 1 small fresh chilli, finely chopped)
- 25g coriander, finely chopped
- 1 carrot, cut into batons
- 6cm cucumber, cut into batons
- 1 yellow pepper, cut into batons

Directions:

1. Preheat the oven to 190°C/ gas mark 5.
2. Roast the peppers and onions for 25-30 minutes, turning occasionally to ensure even cooking.
3. Remove any charred pieces and discard. Reserve half the peppers and onions, then add the other half to a blender with the tomatoes, tomato puree, cumin, oregano and chilli flakes. blend until smooth.
4. Chop the rest of the onion and red pepper, then stir into the blended ingredients along with the fresh coriander. Stir in the remaining ingredients and serve with the vegetable sticks.

Recipe Tips

You could use any colour peppers. Also delicious served with pitta bread fingers.

The salsa also works well as an accompaniment to grilled meat or fish. Or try adding some to your favourite sandwich or wrap.

Nutrition:

KCal 65   Carbs 10.6g   Fibre 4.6g   Protein 2.1g   Fat 0.6g   Saturates 0.1g   Sugars 9.6g   Salt 0.04g Fruit/Veg Portion 2

Roasted Peppers With Feta Cheese

Servings: 2

Cooking Time: 30 Minutes

Ingredients:

- 2 peppers, halved and deseeded (1 red and 1 yellow or orange)
- 12 cherry tomatoes
- 8 pitted black olives
- 50g feta cheese, crumbled
- 1 tsp olive oil
- 1 tsp fresh oregano

Directions:

1. Preheat the oven to 200°C/gas 6. Place the peppers on a baking tray, cut side up.
2. Toss together the remaining ingredients and use to fill the peppers.
3. Cook for 30 minutes until the peppers are tender.

Recipe Tips

You could use other cheeses such as goat's cheese, mature cheddar or mozzarella.

Try using baby peppers to create mini versions of this dish (cooking time will reduce to 20 minutes).

Nutrition:

KCal 53   Carbs 9.3g   Fibre 42.0g   Protein 5.9g   Fat 9.3g   Saturates 4.1g   Sugars 8.6g   Salt 0.91g   Fruit/Veg Portion 2

Roasted Garlic And Mushroom Soup

Servings: 4

Cooking Time: 40 Minutes

Ingredients:

- 4 whole bulbs garlic, unpeeled with tops removed
- 2 tsp rapeseed oil
- 1 large onion, chopped
- 2 large Portobello mushrooms, sliced (150g)
- 200g closed cup mushrooms, sliced
- 1 reduced-salt vegetable stock cube in 500ml water
- good pinch white pepper
- half tsp dried thyme
- 1 400g can cannellini beans, drained
- 100ml skimmed milk
- 150g mixed exotic or wild mushrooms
- 3 tbsp 0% fat Greek-style yogurt
- black pepper to taste
- fresh thyme leaves, to serve (optional)

Directions:

1. Place the garlic on a square of kitchen foil and rub with a teaspoon of the oil. Fold into a package and bake in the oven 190°C/gas mark 5 for 30-35 minutes.
2. Add the rest of the oil to a pan, then add the onion and cook for 5-6 minutes, stirring regularly until browned.

3. Next, add the sliced cup and Portobello mushrooms, then continue cooking for a further 5 minutes until softened. Add the stock, pepper and dried thyme, mix well, bring to the boil, then turn down the heat. Add a lid and simmer gently for 5 minutes.

4. Squeeze the garlic out of the skin and add to the saucepan along with the cannellini beans and bring back to the boil. Add the milk, blend, and reserve.

5. Meanwhile, sauté the wild mushrooms in a non-stick pan for 3-4 minutes and reserve.

6. Add the yogurt to the soup, blend well, then divide into 4 bowls. Top with the sautéed wild mushrooms, a good grind of black pepper and fresh thyme leaves.

Recipe Tips

You can use any combination of mushrooms for this soup. Also works well with other beans, such as butter beans.

Try with basil or oregano in place of thyme.

Roasting the garlic makes it much milder and sweeter, so don't be put off by the amount you're using.

Freezing instructions: Suitable for freezing once cooked. Stir in the sautéed mushrooms before freezing. Defrost in a microwave or over a very low heat until piping hot.

Nutrition:

KCal 172   Carbs 21.1g   Fibre 7.6g   Protein 11.6g   Fat 2.9g   Saturates 0.2g   Sugars 6.1g   Salt 0.22g   Fruit/Veg Portion 1

Tomato Bagels

Servings: 2

Cooking Time: 10 Minutes

Ingredients:

- 4 medium vine tomatoes, halved
- 1 tsp rapeseed oil
- 1 large leek, shredded
- 2 wholemeal bagels
- 60g fat-free Quark
- 3 tsp fresh chives, chopped and 1 tsp to garnish
- freshly ground black pepper

Directions:

1. Heat the grill, and place the tomatoes onto a baking sheet, cut-side down. Grill for 3-4 minutes, then turn over and grill for a further 3-4 minutes until slightly browned.

2. Meanwhile, add the leeks to a microwave proof dish with a teaspoon of water, cover with film and cook on full power for 2-3 minutes until soft, allow to cool a little and drain off any excess liquid.

3. Cut the bagels in half, toast, then spread with cream cheese and scatter with leek. Place 3 tomato halves on one bagel half, sprinkle with chives and black pepper, then top with another bagel half. Repeat with the other bagel.

4. Top each with a little cream cheese, another tomato half and a little leek then garnish with the remaining chives and black pepper.

Recipe Tips

Try adding cottage cheese or, for a vegan bagel, use a

non-dairy alternative.

Experiment with different herbs such as basil, or try rubbing the toasted bagel with a clove of garlic.

Also delicious with grilled mushrooms in place of tomatoes.

Nutrition:

KCal 329   Carbs 48.9g   Fibre 10.1g   Protein 16.3g

Fat 5.4g   Saturates 0.7g   Sugars 13.6g   Salt 0.75g

Fruit/Veg Portion 3

Tomato And Red Pepper Risotto

Servings: 2

Cooking Time: 20-25 Minutes

Ingredients:

- 1 tbsp rapeseed oil
- 1 small onion, finely chopped
- 100g risotto rice
- 400g tin plum tomatoes, juice and flesh puréed
- 150ml low-salt vegetable stock
- 1 tbsp fresh Parmesan cheese, grated
- 400g tin pimentos, drained and flesh sliced
- freshly ground black pepper

Directions:

1. Heat the oil in a non-stick pan. Add the onion and fry for 2-3 minutes until softened.

2. Stir in the rice and coat in the oil. Pour in the tomatoes and stock, bring to the boil and simmer gently for 15-20 minutes, stirring continuously, until the rice is just tender.

3. Stir through the remaining ingredients, season well,

heat through and serve.

Recipe Tips

Keep a kettle of boiling water handy. If the risotto starts to stick you can add a dash of water. As long as you use boiling water, it won't stop the rice from cooking as you add it.

Stirring a risotto constantly during cooking helps make it more creamy.

Freezing instructions: Suitable for freezing once cooked. Chill quickly. Defrost in the fridge and reheat thoroughly until piping-hot throughout. Eat immediately and discard any leftovers.

Nutrition:

KCal 385   Carbs 56.3g   Fibre 3.4g   Protein 12.4g

Fat 11.5g   Saturates 3.6g   Sugars 13.9g   Salt 1.1g

Fruit/Veg Portion 4

Tofu Noodle Stir Fry

Servings: 4

Cooking Time: 10 Minutes

Ingredients:

- 225g block firm tofu
- oil spray
- 2 long shallots, peeled and sliced
- 2 orange peppers, sliced
- 2.5cm piece fresh ginger, finely chopped
- 225g pack baby corn, carrots and mangetout
- 225g beansprouts
- 225g straight-to-wok noodles
- 1 tbsp reduced-salt soy sauce

- freshly ground black pepper

Directions:

1. Drain the tofu and pat dry with kitchen paper. Cut into bite-sized pieces and season with freshly ground black pepper.

2. Heat a non-stick wok. Lightly spray with oil and add the tofu. Stir-fry quickly over a high heat, stirring until lightly browned. Transfer to a plate.

3. Add the shallots and peppers to the wok and stir-fry over a high heat. Add the ginger, baby corn, carrots and mangetout, stir-fry for 2-3 minutes. Add the beansprouts and stir-fry for 2 minutes.

4. Fold in the noodles and soy sauce until heated through. Return the tofu to the work and stir well. Serve immediately.

Recipe Tips

For extra flavour, add one or two crushed garlic cloves or 1 tsp Chinese 5 Spice powder.

You could use 200g chicken, turkey or fish in place of tofu.

Use rice to make this recipe gluten-free.

Nutrition:

KCal 175   Carbs 22.0g   Fibre 6.2g   Protein 10.8g
Fat 3.5g   Saturates 0.5g   Sugars 8.9g   Salt 1.22g
Fruit/Veg Portion 2

Tofu Stuffed Mushrooms

Servings: 2

Cooking Time: 30 Minutes

Ingredients:

- 2 large Portobello mushrooms, stems removed and reserved
- 1 tsp rapeseed oil
- 3 spring onions, finely chopped
- 150g firm tofu, finely chopped
- 100g frozen spinach, defrosted and water squeezed out
- good pinch black pepper
- 2 tsp tahini
- 1 tsp Dijon mustard
- 1 tbsp fresh basil, chopped
- 6 cherry tomatoes, chopped

Directions:

1. Preheat oven to 180°C / gas mark 4. Place the mushroom caps (top-side down) onto a lightly-oiled baking sheet.

2. Heat oil in a large pan over a medium heat, then finely chop the mushroom stems and add to the pan with the spring onions and tofu.

3. Cook for 3-4 minutes, then add the spinach and pepper and cook for 2-3 minutes, mixing regularly.

4. Remove from the heat and mix in the tahini, mustard and basil.

5. Mound each mushroom with the tofu mixture and bake for 15- 20 minutes. Top with chopped tomatoes and serve.

Recipe Tips

You can use leeks in place of spring onions and parsley rather than basil.

Spice it up with a pinch of chilli flakes or a teaspoon of smoked paprika.

You could also stuff halved peppers in place of mushrooms

Freezing instructions: The mushrooms are suitable for freezing once cooked. Wrap individually in greaseproof paper and without the chopped tomatoes. Defrost for 2 hours, then warm in the microwave or a moderate oven.

Nutrition:

KCal 179   Carbs 3.6g   Fibre 4.4g   Protein 15.1g   Fat 10.6g   Saturates 1.5g   Sugars 3.1g   Salt 0.14g   Fruit/Veg Portion 2

Tasty Layered Potatoes

Servings: 4

Cooking Time: 1 Hour

Ingredients:

- 1.25kg thinly sliced potatoes
- 3 cloves sliced garlic
- 1 tbsp fresh thyme
- 2 tbsp olive oil

Directions:

1. In a large lightly greased ovenproof dish, layer the sliced potatoes, sliced garlic and fresh thyme.

2. Mix together the olive oil and 200ml water, season and pour over the potatoes.

3. Cover with foil and bake at 170°C/gas 3, for 1 hour,

removing the foil halfway through cooking time.

Recipe Tips

You could also layer with thinly sliced onions.

For extra flavour, use stock instead of water or top with a little grated Cheddar cheese when you remove the foil.

You can do this with other root veg like swede or sweet potatoes.

Suitable for freezing once cooked. Defrost in the fridge or microwave and reheat until piping hot throughout.

Nutrition:

KCal 301   Carbs 51.7g   Fibre 5.7g   Protein 6.9g   Fat 6.2g   Saturates 0.9g   Sugars 1.8g   Salt 0.06g   Fruit/Veg Portion 0

Tartiflette (Breakfast Stir-Fry)

Servings: 2

Cooking Time: approx 35 Minutes

Ingredients:

- 150g baby potatoes
- 2 tsp rapeseed oil
- 150g button mushrooms, quartered
- 6 spring onions, trimmed and chopped into 1cm pieces
- 1 heaped tsp plain flour
- 150ml skimmed milk
- 30g mature Cheddar, grated
- black pepper, to season

Directions:

1. Boil the potatoes whole in their skins for 15–25 minutes, depending on their size. Drain, then cut

into a mixture of halves and quarters.

2. Heat the rapeseed oil in a large frying pan and add the potatoes. Cook, turning regularly, for 3 minutes.

3. Add the mushrooms to the pan with the potatoes and cook, stirring, for another 3 minutes, then add the spring onions and cook, stirring, for a further 2 minutes.

4. Sprinkle the flour over everything and stir to mix well. Next, gradually pour in the milk, stirring constantly, for 2–3 minutes.

5. Stir in the cheese, season with pepper and serve.

Nutrition:

KCal 210   Carbs 21.1g   Fibre 3.1g   Protein 10.2g   Fat 8.7g   Saturates 3.6g   Sugars 8.6g   Salt 0.38g Fruit/Veg Portion 1

Sweet Potato Pudding Cake

Servings: 8

Cooking Time: 2 Hours 15 Minutes

Ingredients:

- 900g sweet potatoes, peeled and chopped
- 25g butter
- 100g soft dark-brown sugar
- grated zest and juice 1 lime
- 4 eggs
- 4 tbsp skimmed milk
- half tsp ground cinnamon
- half tsp ground nutmeg
- 2 tsp baking powder
- 75g raisins

Directions:

Preheat the oven to 180ºC/gas 4. Place the sweet potatoes in a large pan, cover with water and cook for 20–25 minutes, until tender. Drain and mash well, cool a little then stir through the butter, sugar and lime zest and juice.

In a separate dish, beat together the remaining ingredients, and stir into the sweet potato mixture.

Grease and line a 900g (18cm x 8cm deep) loaf tin. Turn mixture into the tin and bake for approx 1½–1¾ hours until firm.

Check the firmness by inserting a skewer – it should come out clean when the dish is cooked.

Recipe Tips

You could also put the mixture into individual ramekins/dishes and bake for around 45 mins.

Keeps in the fridge for up to 5 days. Warm up a slice and serve with reduced-fat crème fraiche or yogurt.

If you don't want to use rum, use 3 tbsp lemon juice instead.

Nutrition:

KCal 249   Carbs 41.8g   Fibre 3.8g   Protein 5.7g   Fat 5.7g   Saturates 2.5g   Sugars 24.7g   Salt 0.61g

Sweet Potato Latkes With Apple Sauce

Servings: 12

Cooking Time: 15-20 Minutes

Ingredients:

- 1 large sweet potato (approx. 350g), peeled
- 1 small onion, finely chopped
- 1 egg, beaten
- good pinch of pepper
- 50g plain flour
- For the sauce:
- 2 apples, peeled, cored and chopped
- 3 tbsp water
- 2 tsp rapeseed oil, to fry

Directions:

1. Grate the sweet potato. Add to a bowl with the onion, egg and pepper, and mix well.

2. Add the flour, mix thoroughly and set aside for 5 minutes.

3. Meanwhile, add the chopped apples and water to a pan with a lid, and cook over a medium to low heat, stirring occasionally and mashing with the back of a spoon. Cook for 12–15 minutes until the apples are soft, then set aside.

4. Heat a non-stick frying pan over a medium heat, add a teaspoon of the oil and spread to coat the base of the pan. When the pan is hot, add a spoonful of the sweet potato mixture and flatten it out into a pancake shape. Cook for 3 minutes, then carefully flip with a spatula and cook on the other side for 2-3 minutes.

5. Serve with the apple sauce.

Recipe Tips

For a lower-sugar accompaniment, these latkes would also taste great served with 0% fat Greek yogurt.

Nutrition:

KCal 68   Carbs 11.9g   Fibre 1.7g   Protein 1.6g   Fat 1.2g   Saturates 0.2g   Sugars 4.2g   Salt 0.05g   Fruit/Veg Portion 0

Sweet Pepper Pancakes With Tangy Tomato Relish

Servings: 30

Cooking Time: 18 Minutes

Ingredients:

- 2 tsp rapeseed oil
- 1 yellow pepper, thinly sliced in 2-3cm lengths
- 1 red pepper, thinly sliced in 2-3cm lengths
- 1 onion, finely chopped
- 2 eggs, beaten
- 200ml water
- 2 tbsp low-fat yogurt
- 50g grated Cheddar cheese
- 150g wholemeal flour
- good pinch pepper
- For the relish:
- 10g fresh parsley
- juice and zest 1 lime
- 4 large vine tomatoes, finely chopped

- 1-2 small red chilies, finely chopped

Directions:

1. Add 1 tsp oil to a pan over a medium heat, add the peppers and onion and cook for 10 minutes, stirring regularly.

2. Meanwhile, mix together the egg, water, yogurt and cheese. Stir in the flour to make a batter.

3. Stir the peppers and onion into the batter.

4. Add the remaining oil to a large non-stick pan. Add scant dessertspoons of the mixture to the pan to fry for 1-2 minutes, flipping once with a spatula to cook the other side for a further minute.

5. Meanwhile, make the sauce by blending together the parsley, lime, zest and fresh tomato together then mix in the chilli.

Recipe Tips

When cooking the pancakes, make sure you distribute the peppers and onion evenly throughout the mixture. You can make them up to 1 day in advance and warm in the oven for a few minutes to serve.

Nutrition:

KCal 39   Carbs 4.6g   Fibre 1.0g   Protein 1.8g   Fat 1.3g   Saturates 0.5g   Sugars 1.2g   Salt 0.05g Fruit/Veg Portion 0

Printed in Great Britain
by Amazon

37698174R00064